Great Expectations

Open Guides to Literature

Series Editor: Graham Martin (Professor of Literature, The Open University)

Current titles

Graham Holderness: *Wuthering Heights*
P.N. Furbank: Pound
Graham Martin: *Great Expectations*
Roderick Watson: MacDiarmid

Titles in preparation

Angus Calder: Byron
David Pirie: Shelley
Walford Davies: Dylan Thomas
Roger Day: Larkin
Jeanette King: *Jane Eyre*
Dennis Walder: Hughes

GRAHAM MARTIN

Great Expectations

Open University Press
Milton Keynes · Philadelphia

Open University Press
Open University Educational Enterprises Limited
12 Cofferidge Close
Stony Stratford
Milton Keynes MK11 1BY, England
and
242 Cherry Street
Philadelphia, PA 19106, USA

First Published 1985

British Library Cataloguing in Publication Data
Martin, Graham, *1927–*
Great expectations.—(Open guides to literature)
1. Dickens, Charles, *1812–1870.* Great expectations
I. Title
823'.8 PR4560

ISBN 0–335–15089–6
ISBN 0–335–15080–2 Pbk

Typeset by Marlborough Design, Oxford
Printed in Great Britain by J.W. Arrowsmith Ltd, Bristol

Contents

Series Editor's Preface

The intention of this series is to provide short introductory books about major writers, texts, and literary concepts for students of courses in Higher Education which substantially or wholly involve the study of Literature.

The series adopts a pedagogic approach and style similar to that of Open University material for Literature courses. *Open Guides* aim to inculcate the reading 'skills' which many introductory books in the field tend, mistakenly, to assume that the reader already possesses. They are, in this sense, 'teacherly' texts, planned and written in a manner which will develop in the reader the confidence to undertake further independent study of the topic. They are 'open' in two senses. First, they offer a three-way tutorial exchange between the writer of the *Guide*, the text or texts in question, and the reader. They invite readers to join in an exploratory discussion of texts, concentrating on their key aspects and on the main problems which readers, coming to the texts for the first time, are likely to encounter. The flow of a *Guide* 'discourse' is established by putting questions for the reader to follow up in a tentative and searching spirit, guided by the writer's comments, but not dominated by an over-arching and single-mindedly-pursued argument or evaluation, which itself requires to be 'read'.

Guides are also 'open' in a second sense. They assume that literary texts are 'plural', that there is no end to interpretation, and that it is for the reader to undertake the pleasurable task of discovering meaning and value in such texts. *Guides* seek to provide, in compact form, such relevant biographical, historical and cultural information as bears upon the reading of the text, and they point the reader to a selection of the best available critical discussions of it. They are not in themselves concerned to propose, or to counter, particular readings of the texts, but rather to put *Guide* readers in a position to do that for themselves. Experienced travellers learn to dispense with guides, and so it should be for readers of this series.

This *Open Guide* is best used in conjunction with the Penguin edition of *Great Expectations* (ed. Angus Calder, 1965); page references given in the text are to this edition. Chapter references are also provided for the convenience of readers using a different edition.

Graham Martin

Acknowledgements

My thanks go the The Open University for permission to develop this book for material originally contributed to their course entitled *The Nineteenth Century Novel and Its Legacy*; to Open University colleagues from whose comments the early drafts of that material so greatly benefited; and especially to Dr Dennis Walder for specific suggestions about developing it in its present form.

1. Contextual

Any literary work published (let us say) more than half a century ago presents its readers with a paradox. On the one hand, we want to read it as a work of our own time, which speaks directly to us today, not as an antiquarian curiosity. On the other hand, we soon find out that it bears evident signs of its own time, the impress of past literary traditions and models, of older publishing practices, of cultural and social influences that to us are 'history'; while in some cases, there will be an autobiographical dimension to the work, as well as the fact that it holds a particular place in the writer's total *œuvre*. Certain aspects of the work will therefore remain enigmatic, even inaccessible, unless we learn something of this context of its original production. But when is the right time to absorb such knowledge? Before reading the work itself, or after? Planning this *Guide* to Dickens's *Great Expectations* raises these questions in a severely practical form: should we start with the 'text', or with the 'context'? There are good arguments either way. Starting with the 'text' at once engages our primary interest, and matters of 'context' are of only modest value on their own. Yet starting with the 'context' has this to be said for it: information is at once available to those readers who like to come to the novel with a preliminary sense of when and how and why it was written. So this first chapter of the *Guide* assembles some of the principal contextual material that literary scholarship has made available to modern readers of Dickens, and which bears in various ways upon a reading of *Great Expectations*. Readers who prefer to kick off with the novel itself should therefore turn now to Chapter 2, and return to this chapter at a later stage.

Genesis and publication

Dickens began *Great Expectations* in September 1860. The idea for it seems to have arisen out of a sketch for one of the short essays he was then contributing to his weekly magazine *All the Year Round* (later collected in *The Uncommercial Traveller*, 1861). He wrote to his friend John Forster (1812–76):

> For a little piece I have been writing – or am writing; for I hope to finish it today – such a very fine, new, and grotesque idea has opened upon me, that I begin to doubt whether I had not better cancel the little paper, and reserve the notion for a new book. You shall judge as soon as I get it printed. But it so opens out before *me* that I can see the whole of a serial revolving on it, in a most singular and comic manner.[1]

At first he intended it for serial publication in twenty monthly numbers, his usual practice. But a crisis in the affairs of *All the Year Round* made him change his mind. The magazine's circulation was suffering badly because of the unpopularity of a serial by Charles Lever (1806–72) called *A Day's Ride*. Early in October, Dickens decided it could only be rescued by contributing a serial of his own. So *Great Expectations* was re-planned in weekly instalments, making its first appearance on 1 December 1860. Once under way with the novel, Dickens wrote again to Forster, explaining its basic idea:

> I have put a child and a good-natured foolish man in relations that seem to me very funny. Of course, I have got in the pivot on which the story will turn too – and which indeed, as you remember, was the grotesque tragi-comic conception that first encouraged me. To be quite sure I had fallen into no unconscious repetitions, I read *David Copperfield* again the other day, and was affected by it to a degree you would hardly believe.[2]

David Copperfield (1849–50) was the novel in which Dickens had already treated, in veiled form, aspects of his own life (see pp. 14–16).

During the winter and spring of 1860–61, he continued to work on the novel, reporting in April that 'two months more will see me through it, I trust. All the iron is in the fire, and I have "only" to beat it out'.[3] Early in June he finished it in its original form, but re-wrote the conclusion in deference to his friend Bulwer Lytton's advice, when he showed him the proofs later in the month.[4] The final instalment appeared in *All the Year Round* on 3 August 1861. The circulation of the magazine had responded gratifyingly, rising several thousands higher than that of *The Times*.

Great Expectations first appeared in book form in 1861, in a three-volume edition published by Chapman and Hall. It went to four editions within a few weeks of publication. There were no illustrations (although some were added to an edition of 1885, and appear in many modern reprints).

Most editors have reprinted the text from an edition of Dickens's novels published in 1867–68. Angus Calder, the editor of the Penguin edition of 1965, has based his text on the original 1861 edition, incorporating some readings from the weekly parts, and from the 1868 edition where it was clear that Dickens had made deliberate changes. Calder's edition is also useful for other reasons. He asterisks the points where each weekly instalment ended. He includes many informative notes, the original conclusion and Dickens's manuscript notes for the final episodes (Appendix A), and the author's notes on the ages of the characters (Appendix B).

Literary influences

As a small boy Dickens read widely in eighteenth-century literature. There is a passage in *David Copperfield* based on Dickens's boyhood years, when he had access to his father's collection of cheap reprints of well-known novels:

> *Roderick Random, Peregrine Pickle, Humphrey Clinker, Tom Jones, The Vicar of Wakefield, Don Quixote, Gil Blas*, and *Robinson Crusoe* . . . They kept alive my fancy . . . they and the *Arabian Nights* and the *Tales of the Genii* – and did me no harm, for whatever harm was in some of them, was not there for me; *I* knew nothing of it. (Chapter 4)

Such works made a permanent impression. *Robinson Crusoe* excepted, the eighteenth-century titles by Smollett, Fielding and Goldsmith are all in the 'picaresque' tradition, in which the story follows the adventures of a principal character, often an outsider in his society, journeying from place to place, meeting all sorts and conditions of men. Dickens's novel, *Pickwick Papers* (1836–7), uses this formula, and few of his novels are unaffected by it. Other important traits can be traced to eighteenth-century models. Like Henry Fielding, Dickens liked to build up a broad social canvas by drawing in a large number of minor characters in different walks of life. Again like Fielding, he approached society as a satirical moralist, but his later novels seem to have been affected by novelists such as Charlotte Brontë (who pioneered the first-person novel in *Jane Eyre*), and George Eliot, both of whom developed the exploration of the inner life begun by Samuel Richardson, the other major eighteenth-century novelist. The handling of Pip in *Great Expectations* is a case in point.

Fielding himself began his career as a comic dramatist and his approach to characterization is directly linked with a stage tradition stretching back to the satirical comedy of the Renaissance dramatist Ben Jonson (an author Dickens admired): for example, the two minor characters in *Tom Jones* called Thwackum and Square were satirical versions of a cleric and a philosopher. Dickens's wonderful series of satirized characters – Pecksniff, Chadband, Mrs Jellyby, Bounderby, Mrs Sparsit, Podsnap – develops this vein. Dickens is also more generally indebted to theatrical traditions. He tends to handle whole scenes 'theatrically' – or, as one is inclined to say when they don't come off, 'stage-ily' – and the dialogue often reflects this.

> 'So proud, so proud!' moaned Miss Havisham, pushing away her grey hair with both her hands.
>
> 'Who taught me to be proud?' returned Estella. 'Who praised me when I learnt my lesson?'
>
> 'So hard, so hard!' moaned Miss Havisham, with her former action.
>
> 'Who taught me to be hard?' returned Estella. 'Who praised me when I learnt my lesson?'
>
> 'But to be proud and hard to *me*!' Miss Havisham quite shrieked, as she stretched out her arms. 'Estella, Estella, Estella, to be proud and hard to *me*!' (Chapter 38, p. 323)

Miss Havisham is, of course, a histrionic character, but Dickens's imagination runs naturally to striking confrontations, large gestures, rhetorical speech, intense moments of revelation and suspense, and to the kinds of characters and situations that supply them.

Perhaps to speak of 'theatrical influence' is to put the cart before the horse. Dickens was interested in the theatre all his life. As a young man, he seriously thought of training for the professional stage. As a successful novelist, he wrote for and acted in amateur theatricals. At the peak of his career, he developed a one-man theatrical representation of famous scenes – comic, pathetic, melodramatic – in popular readings from his own novels. One critic has argued that his novels are always essentially 'theatrical', and remarks of *Great Expectations*:

> The great virtuoso [i.e. Dickens] appears on stage in the theatrical disguise of a man called Philip Pirrip who purports to be telling us his story, reporting his observations of men and manners, and moralizing on his own career. This illusion – that we are hearing a man called Pip speaking to us – is most skilfully contrived to give the impression of consistency, but it gives that impression only to the reader who is at ease with the theatricality of the occasion . . .[5]

The argument is extreme, but it focuses a real issue: the identity of the novel's narrator.

David Copperfield praised the eighteenth-century novelists for keeping alive his *fancy*, and adds the *Arabian Nights* and *Tales of the Genii* to his reading list. Dickens had a nurse who regaled his young mind with fanciful horrors:

> One of these gory narratives concerned a certain Captain Murderer who slaughtered his successive wives, baked them in meat pies, ate them, and picked the bones. Ultimately this sinister character met his just fate through a poison injected into the pie crust by a suspicious victim, which caused him to swell up and turn blue and scream until he filled the room from floor to ceiling and finally burst.[6]

Not a 'literary influence' in the sense usually defined by the academic researcher, but a useful reminder nevertheless both of Dickens's own imaginative vigour, and of its bias towards the grotesque, the macabre, the melodramatic. In the detail of *Great Expectations* you will find examples enough, but you might also consider the more general suggestion of some critics that a fairy-tale element underlies the story: Miss Havisham as the wicked fairy casting her blighting spell on the young hero, Estella the petrified beauty, Satis House the enchanted palace.

Yet clearly Dickens's art is grounded in a kind of 'realism', a necessary term in the discussion of literature, though to be used with care (see my Chapter 4). His literary career was preceded by a spell as a reporter of Parliamentary debates and elections, and he astonished his colleagues by an outstanding combination of accuracy and speed. His first published work, *Sketches by Boz* (1836–37), was a collection of impressionistic reports on contemporary life, distinguished for their fresh and keen observation. *Pickwick Papers* (also 1836–37) combined comic invention with a similar direct record, and his early novels grew out of a conscious interest in immediate social problems observed at first hand. If it is true that Dickens's imagination converts everything it touches, an essential element in the final result is realistic observation of the Victorian world. One of the new things about eighteenth-century novelists was their formulation of experiences for which the polite Augustan literary tradition (e.g. Pope, Addison) had no place: the actual people and emerging social patterns of bustling, commercial, city existence. In this sense Dickens's 'realism' about his own times falls into a literary tradition, even though we can hardly ascribe it to 'literary influence'.

Dickens's later novels are in many respects more carefully thought out, more coherently planned than those that established his fame. Many critics think *Great Expectations* his most satisfying in this respect, without loose ends, extravagant digressions or over-ingenious complication. We can see this from Dickens's use of the 'picaresque' device, the journeyings of the hero as the thread on which various other stories and characters are hung. This is perhaps one clue to the structure of *Great Expectations*. Dickens adapts the simplest kind of 'picaresque' – Tom Jones's travels from Somerset to London, Humphrey Clinker's wanderings, Mr Pickwick's rural cavorting – to more complex use.

Serialization

When Dickens began to write in the mid-1830s, it was the usual practice of novelists to publish a single work in three or four volumes, each costing perhaps as much as half a guinea. Jane Austen's and Sir Walter Scott's novels appeared in this form: *Mansfield Park* (1814) was a 'three-decker', as three-volume novels were nicknamed, which sold at 10*s.* 6*d.* a volume. Most probably Dickens's novels would have been published in the same way, but for the enormous success of *Pickwick Papers*. This originally appeared serially, in illustrated monthly parts consisting of three or four chapters apiece, costing a shilling – 'a low, cheap form of publication', Dickens was later to observe, which he associated with 'certain interminable novels . . . carried about the country by pedlars, and over some of which I remember to have shed innumerable tears, before I served my apprenticeship to Life'.[7] This scheme originated with the publishers, and Dickens's text – he was then a little-known journalist – was mainly to be the vehicle for humorous illustrations on a subject already decided by an established illustrator. So Dickens took up the work without a preconceived plan, and because it was unusually well paid. But in the event his development of the story and the characters assumed a dominant role and as the monthly issues piled up, gained him his reputation for unrivalled comic invention, keen observation of the contemporary world and vigorous satire on its evils. *Pickwick's* extraordinary popularity may be judged from a comparison of the expected sale of about four hundred copies a month with the actual sale for the third month of about five hundred, and for the twelfth of *forty thousand*. But equally important as this financial success was Dickens's early realization that serial publication suited his creative powers. After only nine numbers of *Pickwick* he began *Oliver Twist* (1837–38) on a similar basis, writing both novels concurrently for nearly a year, and before finishing *Oliver* he began *Nicholas Nickleby* (1838–39). In all he published eight novels in monthly form. He also published five novels, of which *Great Expectations* is one, in weekly instalments in one or other of his magazines *Household Words* and *All the Year Round*.

Two general points arise from Dickens's use of serial publication, concerning: (a) his relationship with his readers, and (b) the planning and structure of the novels.[8]

Serialization and the novelist's readers

Serial publication allowed the development of a special reciprocal relationship between Dickens and his readers. From the relative sales of monthly numbers he discovered the best way to present his ideas. Thus the sales of *Pickwick* only began to rise when he introduced the comic character of Sam Weller in the fifth number, and rose more steeply when, with Mr Pickwick's imprisonment, a new vein of social satire entered the novel. This concurrence between Dickens's creative instincts and the taste of his readers was at least one of the factors which enabled him to attack contemporary social evils with such trenchant confidence. But this attunement with his readers was equally important for them. Serial novels build up a stronger illusion of 'reality' than most fiction (as many contemporary TV serials indicate). Here is a contemporary reaction to one number of *The Old Curiosity Shop* (1840–41), Lady Stanley, writing to a friend about the villain's death:

> How *can* you read [the] last number and not *indulge* me with an ejaculation or two about it? Are you satisfied with the disposal of Quilp? My Lord is not, says it is too easy a death and that he should have more time to *feel* his punishment. Will Nelly die? I think she ought.[9]

The prospect of Little Nell's death was so keenly felt that as the first copies of the final number approached New York, it is said that crowds assembled on the pier, desperate to know her end.

An article published after Dickens's death put the matter this way:

> The obvious effect [of serial publication] was to inspire all his constant readers – say, a million or two – with a sense of habitual dependence on their contemporary, the man Charles Dickens, for a continued supply of the entertainment he alone could furnish. He was personally indispensable to them, as a favourite actor might be to the inveterate playgoers of a former age, who lived upon their Garrick or their Kemble.[10]

This writer did not choose his theatrical comparison casually. In the final years of his career Dickens gave public readings from his novels which expressed not only his lifelong interest in acting and the theatre, but also a continuing need for a direct relationship with his readers, which by that time the familiar serial form no longer satisfied.

Another point about Dickens's readers should be mentioned. He helped to create a new audience for serious fiction by bringing the price within the range of readers other than the aristocracy and the wealthier middle class, who could afford the high cost of a new three-volume novel. His own audience extended throughout the social hierarchy, as far as the illiterate. A contemporary came upon

> a group of twenty men and women who were too poor to afford the shilling that would buy a monthly part [of *Pickwick Papers*] and who were renting a copy at two-pence a day from a circulating library, which one of them read aloud to the others.[11]

There is some evidence that the illustrations were designed to highlight key themes for those who couldn't read.[12] Quite apart from the particular social causes for which Dickens from time to time campaigned in his novels, we need to remember that in a much more pervasive way he articulated for such readers a sense of contemporary reality, as did no other novelist of his time. This putting into words, images and stories the dim feelings and barely conceived thoughts shared by sizeable groups of people whose experience, by and large, had *not* been catered for in cultural consciousness was a socially creative act of the first importance. Dickens's radicalism took several forms, but it is arguable that his successful development of serial publication was the most influential.

Moreover, within a few years of *Pickwick* the 'low, cheap form of publication' had become generally acceptable. Thackeray, Trollope, George Eliot, James and Hardy all used it for major novels. As well as creating a more varied audience for his own work, Dickens thus helped to make more generally available that of other novelists who themselves would probably not have chosen serial publication. Shortly before he wrote *Great Expectations*, Dickens suggested to George Eliot that she publish *Adam Bede* (1859) in weekly instalments in *All the Year Round*, but she decided this would not be suitable for the novel's leisurely, meditative pace. But her *Middlemarch* (1871–72) appeared in eight bi-monthly instalments and *Daniel Deronda* (1876) in eight monthly instalments. After the last number had appeared, Henry James wrote a dialogue discussion in which a character remarks:

> A book like *Daniel Deronda* becomes part of one's life: one lives in it, or alongside it. I don't hesitate to say that I have been living in this one for the last eight months. It is such a complete world George Eliot builds up; it is so vast, so much-embracing. It has such a firm earth and such an ethereal sky. You can turn into it and lose yourself in it.[13]

Perhaps this is an effect of all major works of literature, but serial publication powerfully contributes to it.

Serialization and the structure of the novel

Serial publication also imposed special demands on the novelist's ability to plan a work whose individual parts would both hold the interest of his readers on 'cliff-hanger' lines, yet still add up to a coherent single novel. Each monthly or weekly number required its quota of incident, varied interest, relative unity, and intelligible but still forward-looking conclusion. Lengthy character analysis and scene-setting became more difficult to bring off. The novelist had to contend with the monthly interval between numbers when readers might forget, or too vaguely remember, important details and effects. For severely practical reasons, systematic planning was also necessary. Monthly deadlines had to be met, time provided for the illustrator to work up his instructions, and length itself could always give problems if the chosen part of the story exceeded or fell short of the regular monthly requirement, as actual composition often proved. A reviewer of *David Copperfield* commented:

> The serial tale . . . is probably the lowest artistic form yet invented; that, namely, which affords the greatest excuse for unlimited departures from dignity, propriety, consistency, completeness, and proportion. In it, wealth is too often wasted in reckless and riotous profusion, and poverty is concealed by superficial variety, caricature, violence, and confused bustle. Nine-tenths of its readers will never look at it or think of it as a whole. A level number, however necessary to the story, will be thrown aside like a flat article in a newspaper. No fault will be found with the introduction of any character or any incident however extravagant or irrelevant, if it will amuse for an hour the lounger in the coffee-room or the traveller by railway. With whatever success men of genius may be able to turn this form to their highest purposes, they cannot make it a high form of art, nor can their works in that kind ever stand in the first class of the products of the imagination.[14]

An extreme view, perhaps, but it states the difficulties for the serial novelist who took his art seriously. How did Dickens solve the problem? Two general characteristics of his novels must have been strongly developed by the pressure of serialization, even if it would be a mistake to trace their origins to it. *Pickwick*, as we've seen, was begun without an overall plan, but for later novels there is plenty of evidence of extended brooding on the main theme, of preliminary designs, and of month-by-month planning. The key to this planning was usually the strong narrative line provided by the 'mystery' plot. This appears in many of his novels as a solution, I would suggest, to the main problem of serialization: how to combine immediate interest with overall unity. Such plots allow for interesting digressions, ambiguous relationships between characters, any amount of complication of detail, intelligent suspense and, above all, a powerful forward movement urging the reader on from number to number towards the final *dénouement*. It doesn't take much experience of reading Dickens to know that what is immediately but *inexplicably* striking will, in the end, be significant in terms of the plot. The impact of single parts is thus correlated with the plans as a whole.

The second point is Dickens's handling of character, especially in the profusion of fascinating minor eccentrics who people most of his novels. The broad, cartoon-like delineation of such characters can be viewed as one of Dickens's ways of combining immediate interest with long-term memorability. Such characters can have needed no re-introduction from number to number. Whether or not they transfer altogether successfully to the completed novel is another matter, which you might think about (e.g. Wopsle).

Dickens often used extensive memoranda to plan the developments of his complicated stories and array of characters for each monthly number. Though no such schemes have survived for *Great Expectations*, some manuscript notes exist on the ages of the characters, on the state of the tides (for Chapter 54), and on the final chapters. Details of the first and third of these are in the Appendices to the Penguin edition.

Dickens's letter to the author of a novel, submitted, in the hope that he might assist its publication, explains the particular demands of weekly serialization. Read it over, and then consider the first two chapters of *Great Expectations*, which made up the first published number of the novel, in the light of the serialization problem. What aspects of these chapters could be said to reflect the appearance of the story in serial form?

> Having gone through your M.S. . . . I write these few following words about it. Firstly, with a limited reference to its unsuitability to these pages. Secondly, with a more enlarged reference to the merits of the story itself.
>
> If you will take any part of it and cut it up (in fancy) into the small

> portions into which it would have to be divided here for only a month's supply, you will (I think) at once discover the impossibility of publishing it in weekly parts. The scheme of the chapters, the manner of introducing the people, the progress of the interest, the places in which the principal incidents fall, are all hopelessly against it. It would seem as though the story were never coming, and hardly ever moving. There must be a special design to overcome that specially trying mode of publication, and I cannot better express the difficulty and labour of it than by asking you to turn over any two weekly numbers of *A Tale of Two Cities*, or *Great Expectations*, or Bulwer's story, or Wilkie Collins', or Reade's, or *At the Bar*, and notice how patiently and expressly the thing has to be planned for presentation in these fragments, and yet for afterwards fusing together as an uninterrupted whole . . .
>
> . . . As a mere piece of mechanical workmanship, I think all your chapters should be shorter; that is to say, that they should be sub-divided. Also, when you change from narrative to dialogue, or vice versa, you should make the transition more carefully. Also, taking the pains to sit down and recall the principal landmarks in your story, you should make them far more elaborate and conspicuous than the rest. Even with these changes I do not believe that the story would attract the attention due to it, if it were published even in such monthly portions as the space of 'Fraser' would admit of. Even so brightened, it would not, to the best of my judgement, express itself piecemeal. It seems to me to be so constituted as to require to be read 'off the reel'. As a book in two volumes I think it would have good claims to success. But I suppose the polishing I have hinted at (not a meretricious adornment, but positively necessary to good work and good art) to have been first thoroughly administered.[15]

In the case of *Great Expectations* it is hardly necessary to mention how striking the first chapter is: the churchyard, Pip's confrontation with the convict, the convict's frightening invention of the young man, and so on. Yet this is also the initiating incident in the mystery of Pip's later life. The second chapter is well contrasted: a domestic scene, humorous in Dickens's painful way, raising enough questions about Pip's circumstances to make the reader curious for more. Notice also that the opening incident is kept steadily in mind, and that the chapter ends in Pip's return to the marshes with the stolen food (about to meet the convict for the second time). There are also some similarities between the two chapters: adults treat Pip violently in both. His orphaned state, which is announced in the first paragraph, is continually underlined by Mrs Joe's resentment at having to bring him up. The characterization of all three adults is vivid and immediate: the convict's fierce desperation, Joe's and Mrs Joe's principal traits of speech and behaviour. (These last two especially will recur.) I would add two other points. A strikingly abrupt beginning is exactly what a new serial needs. Then there is the balance of the two chapters: one is the convict's world – vulnerable, outcast, violent – and one is the law-abiding society which, as the novel goes on to show, is nevertheless far more intimately connected with criminality than it cares to imagine. Pip's life is divided between these two worlds. This is not a connection that the first readers of the serial version could have grasped, but it shows how well this outstanding first number introduces the deeper themes of the whole novel.

Biographical

Great Expectations begins and ends in places connected with Dickens's childhood. Pip's village was probably based on Cooling, a few miles north of Rochester, Kent, which is the original of the nearby market town where Miss Havisham and Pumblechook lived, and where the London coach left from. Satis House was based on an Elizabethan mansion near Rochester Cathedral. Dickens spent his boyhood in Chatham, about a mile from Rochester, and he was again living in the district when he began *Great Expectations*. In 1856 he bought a large house called Gad's Hill Place on the outskirts of Chatham, at the top of a steep hill which he'd often walked up with his father. Owning this house had been a childhood dream. At first he used it as a summer residence, moving back to his London home near Regent's Park in the winter. But in 1858 Dickens separated from his wife, and in the spring of 1860 decided to make Gad's Hill Place his permanent home. It seems not unreasonable to connect the composition of *Great Expectations* with so decided a return to childhood localities. After its publication Dickens would conduct his friends – at his customary punishing four miles an hour – on pedestrian visits to the marsh scenery. His friend and biographer Forster tells us:

> To another drearier churchyard, itself forming part of the marshes beyond the Medway, he often took friends to show them the dozen small tombstones of various sizes adapted to the respective ages of a dozen small children of the family which he made part of his story. . . About the whole of this Cooling churchyard, indeed, and the neighbouring castle ruins, there was a weird strangeness that made it one of his attractive walks in the late year or winter, when from Higham he could get to it across country over the stubble fields.[16]

'. . . five little stone lozenges, each about a foot and a half long . . .'
(Chapter 1, page 35)

'. . . he came closer to my tombstone, took me by both arms, and tilted me back as far as he could hold me . . .' (Chapter 1, page 37)

Dickens's separation from his wife was the outcome of a long and deepening estrangement brought to a head by his friendship with a young actress, Ellen Lawless Ternan, whom he had met in 1857. Within a year the acquaintance had ripened sufficiently for it to be freely rumoured that Ellen was Dickens's mistress, though this seems to have been the case only in later years. In his life of Dickens, Edgar Johnson suggests that Pip's relationship with Estella reflects Dickens's interest in Ellen Ternan, on the grounds that it seemed at the time a hopeless love and that *Great Expectations* is his first novel to give a convincing portrayal of a passionate and unrewarded love.[17] Whether this biographical source throws much light on the novel is another matter. Perhaps it is more useful to notice that, if these *are* its origins in Dickens's personal history, then *Great Expectations* has very thoroughly transmuted them into a self-consistent fiction. The relationship between Pip and Estella needs no biographical annotation to be understood.

These matters have their interest, but there is a deeper, more revealing autobiographical note in *Great Expectations*. As we have seen, once started on the composition, Dickens re-read *David Copperfield* to make sure that in his new novel he had not 'fallen into . . . unconscious repetitions' (see p. 2). The two novels are so different that such anxiety seems misplaced until we realize that he was thinking of a particular episode in his young life, the seed of a major crisis. In the earlier novel, Dickens tells how the young David is sent by his cruel stepfather, Mr Murdstone, to work in a bottling warehouse in the Strand, near the present Hungerford Bridge across the Thames. Dickens drew here on memories so bitter that only his close friend and biographer, John Forster, knew about them. In 1823, when Dickens was eleven, money difficulties had forced his father to move the family from Chatham to a poor district in London – Bayham Street, Camden Town. The family's affairs were in chaos, Dickens's father was imprisoned in the Marshalsea Prison for debt, and a relative suggested that young Charles could be usefully employed in a blacking factory in the Strand, by the Hungerford Stairs. The rest of the family moved into the Marshalsea to save expenses, and for a while Dickens seems to have been thrown very much on his own resources. Later, the debts paid and the family re-united, Dickens was taken from the factory job, and eventually his father managed to find him some kind of schooling. Dickens seems never to have forgiven his mother for preferring that he should remain in the blacking factory in order to earn a badly needed wage of seven shillings a week.[18]

From these painful experiences there eventually sprang a major theme of Dickens's writing, that of the abandoned, or orphaned, or maltreated child. A second theme, hardly less important but more diffuse, drew some of its personal significance from the same episode: the lower-middle-class fear of being de-classed. Dickens felt that his weeks in the factory were socially shameful, and it is this aspect that *David Copperfield* avoids mentioning. Not only is David sent to the job by a sadistic stepfather, but he engineers his own escape to the fairy godmother, Aunt Betsy Trotwood, and so to a gentleman's schooling in Canterbury. The taint of the factory never damages David's social position; all its hidden shame is transformed into the moral obloquy attaching to Mr Murdstone for sending him there. In *Great Expectations*, however, Dickens faces the social aspect of his memories more directly. Where David is unjustly banished from his gentleman's birthright to social degradation, but finds his way back to respectable life, Pip starts as a common village boy for whom the onset of class consciousness is eventually seen as a calamity. The gentleman's estate to which he rises turns out both arid and illusory, finally to be rejected in a self-sacrificing act of loyalty towards a repugnant social outcast. It is this act that reconciles Pip with socially humble relatives such as Joe and Biddy. This cutting analysis of Pip's social aspirations can be seen as Dickens's mature judgement on the earlier self that had been so deeply affected by the lure of 'gentility'.

There is a further point about the autobiographical aspect of the novel. In his own life Dickens became a gentleman. He was well off, owned large comfortable houses and was socially famous, not on 'great expectations' but from his own ability, driving energy and – above all – extremely hard work. Economically and socially, his life exemplified a general point about Victorian society that we will discuss more fully (see Chapters 3 and 5). It is worth while asking whether or not *Great Expectations* reflects that aspect of Dickens's life and, if it does, whether this can be reconciled with the novel's insistent paradox that crime and violence are intimately connected with money and respectable success.

I have concentrated here on elements in Dickens's life that are relevant to *Great Expectations*. You will find a brief biographical sketch in Angus Calder's introduction to the Penguin edition, and a full one in the *Dictionary of National Biography*. It is useful, in a general way, to know something about Dickens's life. For the standard biographies, see the sections entitled *Notes* and *Further Reading* (pp. 89 and 91).

2. Formal

As Auden has remarked, there is an element of 'pure contraption' in all poetry, and despite the many differences between the *genres*, the same holds true of novels. Let us begin our joint exploration of *Great Expectations* by concentrating on its 'contraptions', its formal organization, those narrative and character-identifying devices which supply some of the novel's distinctive features, and with which, as readers, we must grapple in our attempts to establish its meaning and value.

Some novelists work hard to conceal the fact that they are writing novels. They strive for an illusion of transparency through which the reader may gaze upon a 'real world'.[1] Is *Great Expectations* like that? If so, how is the illusion brought about? What novelistic tricks and manipulations are responsible for the effect? If not, where is the evidence? Where does Dickens nudge us towards the realization that it *is* a 'fiction', a novel we are reading? If we think of *Great Expectations* as a whole, then there is an explicit statement following the end of Chapter 19, where we find this capitalized sentence:

THIS IS THE END OF THE FIRST STAGE OF PIP'S EXPECTATIONS.

Following Chapter 39, there is a similar sentence about 'The second stage. . .' (p. 342). Each of these pronouncements marks a key moment in Pip's life: in the first case, his departure from London, confident in the belief that Miss Havisham is his secret benefactor; in the second, his discovery of the devastating truth that Abel Magwitch is the real source of his expectations. And if you briefly recall the main events of these 'stages', you'll see at once that they reflect a clear tripartite structure for the novel. Chapters 1–19 tell of Pip's life in his home village, his relationships with his family, and the meetings with Miss Havisham and Estella. Chapters 20–39 are located in London, telling of Pip's life as a 'brought-up London gentleman' (as Magwitch calls him (p. 339)), his contacts with the Pocket family, Herbert, Jaggers, Wemmick, and the hopelessness of his love for Estella. The third and final section resolves the various mysteries, reconciles Pip with his family, tells briefly about his subsequent life, ending with his last meeting with Estella.

Moreover, Dickens's choice of the term 'stage' to mark out the critical periods in Pip's life can hardly have been casual. Journeys have stages, and so do pilgrimages. A life that can be defined by stages must have shape and direction, and the story of such a life is likely to be exemplary, an illustration of some general truth the teller wishes to convey. In English fiction the archetype of such stories is *The Pilgrim's Progress from the World to that which is to come* (1678) by John Bunyan (1622–88), and while I am not suggesting any direct relationship between it and *Great Expectations*,[2] nevertheless, is it not fair to say that Pip's story represents a kind of 'progress', and that Dickens wants us to hold this clearly in mind? We shall come back to this notion of 'Pip's Progress', but meanwhile, the fact that Dickens marks out the tripartite structure in this way seems clear evidence that he wants us to see Pip's story as a 'fiction', a tale, and (so I would suggest) a tale with a moral.

Such a recognition though, you may very well want to say, will be delayed at least till Chapter 19. How, as readers, do we take the chapters themselves before reaching Dickens's piece of narrative signposting? Would you now read over Chapter 1 with the issue of novelistic 'contraptions' in mind? What signs or clues are we given? Are they explicit, or concealed? Or is there a combination of both kinds?

DISCUSSION

The chapter opens with an 'I' telling us his name, how he came by it, the fact that his parents and infant brothers were all dead, then going on to describe their tombstones, the churchyard and surrounding location, and the occasion when he gained his 'first most vivid and broad impression of the identity of things' (p. 35). Now this particular storytelling tactic, variously called first-person narration or pseudo-autobiography, certainly doesn't conceal from us that we are reading a story. On the contrary, it announces the fact. Yet at the same time, by plunging us immediately into one individual's experience of the world, it is remarkably effective in persuading us that the story is 'real'. And so in this case. Three opening paragraphs are addressed to us, explicitly, as readers: 'So, I called myself Pip, and came to be called Pip. I gave Pirrip as my father's family name, on the authority of his tombstone and my sister. . . Ours was the marsh country, down by the river. . .' (p. 35). The narrator is establishing his credentials for the story he is about to tell – name, family, place of residence. But who is the fourth paragraph addressed to?

> 'Hold your noise!' cried a terrible voice, as a man started up from among the graves at the side of the church porch. 'Keep still, you little devil, or I'll cut your throat!' (Chapter 1, p. 36).

These commands and threatenings are, of course, addressed to Pip. Certainly, we understand them as the first event in the story which Pip has set out to tell us. Nevertheless, our relationship with them is not the same as with those first three paragraphs. We are put in the position of being listeners, overhearers, watchers, of speech and events.

Pip, the reporter of the speech, has momentarily disappeared into the language of his report. Hence the effect on us of being 'really present' at the event. And, this is largely the method of the rest of the chapter, Pip reporting what was said to him, done to him, how he felt about it, in such a manner as to present the occasion to us as directly as possible. Our consciousness that we are being told a story has, for the time being, lapsed into the events of the story itself. We participate in these events from Pip's point of view, in relation to his feelings. The 'fearful man' is presented to us externally, a mysterious and terrible irruption into Pip's life, otherwise unexplained. And this, too, contributed to the effect of 'reality': how else, we say, *would*, a child respond to such an event?

I have said that this is *largely* the method of the rest of the chapter, but is it entirely so? For example, do you notice any contrast between the language of these two paragraphs?

> A fearful man, all in coarse grey, with a great iron on his leg. A man with no hat, and with broken shoes, and with an old rag tied round his head. A man who had been soaked in water, and smothered in mud, and lamed by stones, and cut by flints, and stung by nettles, and torn by briars; who limped, and shivered, and glared and growled; and whose teeth chattered in his head as he seized me by the chin. (Chapter 1, p. 36)

> After darkly looking at his leg and me several times, he came closer to my tombstone, took me by both arms, and tilted me back as far as he could hold me; so that his eyes looked most powerfully down into mine, and mine looked most hopelessly up into his. . . He gave me a

> most tremendous dip and roll, so that the church jumped over its own weathercock. Then, he held me by the arms, in an upright position on the top of the stone, and went on in these fearful terms. (Chapter 1, p. 37)

The difference I notice is that the second paragraph is in the reporting manner: 'he came closer . . . tilted me back . . . gave me . . . held me' – we use such verbs when we are reporting something that has happened. But the first paragraph is different. Pip does not say '*I saw* a fearful man . . . etc.', though doubtless we interpret the paragraph in that way. The first two sentences have no verbs, and this brings us immediately up against what Pip *is* seeing. The introductory verb 'I saw' would put the event at a greater distance, would it not? But look at the third sentence: 'a man who *had been soaked*. . .' We move away here from anything that the terrified little Pip could have known at this point to an indirect account of Magwitch's sufferings since his escape from the Hulks. Then there are the several repetitions of 'a man', and the deliberate piling up of detail ('and . . . and . . . and'). Don't we sense here the presence of *writing*, of language being used to convey particular effects upon us as readers? It seems to me that the narrator contrives two effects here: the paragraph maintains the terrifying effect upon the little Pip of the irruption announced in 'Hold your noise!', yet also, less directly, says something about the man responsible for it. That last detail ('he seized me by the chin') returns to the direct report of what Pip was undergoing, but meanwhile, the intervening sentences swerve away from Pip's situation so as to attract sympathy for Magwitch's miserable condition.

So where have we arrived? I asked you to look out for the fictional 'contraptions' which this first chapter might reveal, and consider how far *Great Expectations* established at the outset the kind of novel it was: did it, or not, confess to being 'a story'? My sense is that it does, *and* it doesn't, primarily because first-person narration is a novelistic method peculiarly effective in conceding and hiding at once the 'fictional' status of what we are being told. The same conclusion is suggested by those variations in the language adopted by the narrator. Mostly, he speaks for the young Pip in the mode of 'realism': here is what actually happened, etc. But the paragraph beginning 'a fearful man' interweaves Pip's young impressions with knowledge he did not then possess. Only somebody who knew the whole of Magwitch's story possessed such knowledge, and he is none other than the narrator who introduces himself in the first paragraph with 'I called myself Pip' (p. 35). Who is this narrator? He is, of course, the *adult* Pip, the teller of his own biography, in full command of the history of the 'fearful man' in the churchyard, who has a very particular reason for hinting to the reader that, terrible as Magwitch certainly appeared at the time, there was much else to his situation.

We meet here, then, an instance of what we will discover to be the defining feature of the narrative method in *Great Expectations*: the narrator's dual technique. Formally, and by his own explicit statement, the adult Pip is telling us about the events that shaped his life, notably those in his childhood. Yet, in order to bring these events close to us, he has to present them in terms that correspond to the child that he was. As adult narrator, Pip possesses a full knowledge of these events, yet repeatedly he has to withhold this knowledge so that we, as readers, will enter directly into the experience of the child on whom they impinged and upon whose initial ignorance of their source and meaning the novel absolutely depends. This dual role for the narrator accounts for the way the telling of the story moves back and forth between the poles of what we can call 'presentation' on the one hand, and 'commentary' on the other. The narrator 'presents' the events when, as adult, he wants to withdraw his own interpretive consciousness and to revive for the reader the immediate experience of his childhood self. Whereas, he 'comments' on the significance of such experiences when he wants to direct our attention to a pattern of consequences – social, psychological, moral – which collectively point to the overall 'meaning' of Pip's story. Moreover, when the narrator 'presents' the story he adopts techniques of 'realism' that work to conceal the fact that a novel is what we are reading, and when he 'comments' on events, the opposite effect results: we recognize that we *are* being told an exemplary tale. This is, perhaps, to put the contrast too baldly. As we will see, the method of narration can shift between the two poles of 'presentation' and 'commentary' with speed and subtlety, and in some instances can combine them. Nevertheless, you will find that the broad contrast is worth looking out for as the principal novelistic 'contraption' which Dickens uses in the telling of *Great Expectations*.

As an exercise, you could now usefully look through Chapter 2 for further examples. Are there moments when we become aware, not of the experience of the young Pip, but of the adult narrator? And in the latter case, what does this tell us about the story as a whole?

DISCUSSION

You could argue that whenever Pip makes, or insinuates, judgements about Joe and Mrs Joe we register the presence of the adult commentator. The first three paragraphs of Chapter 2 show this. But there are more explicit cases. Thus: 'Conscience is a dreadful thing when it accuses man or boy; but when, in the case of a boy that secret burden co-operates with another secret burden down the leg of his trousers, it is (as I can testify) a great punishment . . .' (p. 44). And: 'Since that time, which is far enough away now, I have often thought that few people know what secrecy there is in the young, under terror. No matter how unreasonable the terror, so that it be terror . . .' (p. 46). It is in this way that the adult Pip shapes and directs our interest in the experiences of his childhood self. Where, in Chapter 1, Pip has been presented in terms of his altogether understandable fears, here his sense of being a criminal is underlined. Terrified of the convict, whom he now knows to be from the Hulks – where, as Mrs Joe tells him, 'People are put . . . because they murder, and because they rob, and forge, and do all sorts of bad' (p. 46) – Pip himself is about to become a robber of Mrs Joe's pantry. This explicit stress upon Pip's deep sense of guilt, of his having committed a crime and being in some sense complicit with a criminal, is only the first of many such instances.

We have considered in a preliminary way how, as a narrative, *Great Expectations* is conducted. Let us now look at another formal issue, how Dickens presents his characters. First, a word of caution about the very concept 'character'. It is hard to do without such a concept in discussing novels, which typically present us with detailed accounts of men and women and children, who have names, live in particular places, work at certain kinds of job or profession, dress themselves in a distictive style, own property, or lack of it. In his seminal book *The Rise of the Novel* (1957), Ian Watt notes this way of representing people in stories as one of the signs that distinguish *novels* from the earlier narrative form which, in large degree, they replaced – the 'Romance', where for example, we are more likely to meet princes and princesses, ogres and monsters, named perhaps, but not located within a social and economic context that we recognize as familiar, and hence 'real'.[3] Stories that contain 'characters', that is, usually are found in the kind of fiction that aims at 'realism', and so we must see this method of representation as one of realism's principal *conventions*. We have to avoid the assumption that 'characters' are direct reflections, or analogues, of living human beings. A character in a novel is no more than something we build up for ourselves on the basis of certain sentences and paragraphs which occur within the narrative text; and what we need to grasp is the role of such characters within that text, the set of relationships which links the sentences and paragraphs to the text as a whole.

In the case of Dickens's novels, the point needs stressing because of a certain critical tradition for discussing his 'characters'. Thus, E. M. Forster, in his influential *Aspects of the Novel* (1927) distinguishes between 'flat' and 'round' characters (pp. 75–85). 'Flat' characters are, as it were, two-dimensional: immediately striking; memorable, predictable in most of their words and actions, often to be 'summed up in a sentence' (p. 79).[4] Whereas 'round' characters have 'depth', are less formulaic, are capable of change throughout the story, and their words and actions suggest reserves of complexity beyond the needs of the immediate occasion. Using these definitions, Forster proposes that Dickens's novels are full of 'flat' characters, while 'round' characters are fairly rare. I mention this distinction here in order to warn against it, for two reasons. While it has its uses (and Forster's development of it is subtler than my brief summary might suggest), it is dangerously metaphorical (*flat, round*). Using it, we pass too easily from the novelist's words to a selective construction from them. And it is implicitly tendentious. Who would wish to be 'flat' when they might be 'round'?! The implication that 'flat' characters are less interesting than 'round' ones is difficult to resist. The flat/round distinction, in fact, closely resembles the equally common one between 'caricatures' and 'fully-developed characters', the judgement going again in favour of the latter, and if we read *Great Expectations* with such concepts to hand, we won't make much progress. Here, as an example, is a comment on Dickens's *Our Mutual Friend* (1865) from a review by Henry James (1843–1916). He remarks on:

> . . . the limits of Mr Dickens's insight. Insight is, perhaps, too strong a word; for we are convinced that it is one of the chief conditions of his genius not to see beneath the surface of things. If we might hazard a definition of his literary character, we should, accordingly, call him the greatest of superficial novelists.[5]

Do you see the way the metaphorical term *surface* (and its implied opposite of *depth*) links up with the overall judgment upon Dickens limited *insight*? James's argument is that because Dickens sees only the surface of human behaviour, he fails to *see in* to what prompts it, the inner mental and emotional life of self-conscious human purpose.

Let us look at some examples from Chapter 4 in the light of the preceding paragraphs. Consider the way Dickens presents the friends of the Gargerys who turn up for the Christmas dinner. Is the method 'superficial', an observation of surfaces, and does it show limitation of insight?

DISCUSSION

The group in question, Mr Wopsle, Mr and Mrs Hubble, and Uncle Pumblechook are, indeed, all presented in terms of 'surface'; i.e., we get a visual impression of how they look and how they speak, but no direct access to how they think and feel (which is what James means by 'insight'). And it is true that of the first three, little more is offered (though you'll recall that Mr Wopsle turns up several times more in this first section of the novel). But Pumblechook is another case, surely? Presentation of 'surface' is certainly the method:

> a large hard-breathing middle-aged slow man, with a mouth like a fish, dull staring eyes, and sandy hair standing upright on his head, so that he looked as if he had just been all but choked, and had that moment come to. (Chapter 4, pp. 55–6)

In a similar way, his reported conversation adds up to a few predictable formulae (though this trait becomes clear to us only after he has made further appearances in the story). But does this mean we get no impression of the kind of man he is? The conversation at the Christmas dinner prompts Pumblechook to say that if, instead of having the good fortune to be brought up 'by hand' by Mrs Joe and to listen to the improving conversation of Mr Wopsle and himself, Pip had been born as a small pig, in such a case:

> You would have been disposed of for so many shillings according to the market price of the article, and Dunstable the butcher would have come to you as you lay in your straw, and he would have whipped you under his left arm, and with his right he would have tucked up his frock to get a penknife from out of his waistcoat pocket, and he would have shed your blood and had your life. No bringing up by hand then. Not a bit of it! (Chapter 4. p. 58)

On the face of it, this is a ridiculous speculation, typical of its pompous inventor. And indeed Pumblechook is intended largely as a figure of fun – or of farce, which is not quite the same thing. But that doesn't stop Dickens suggesting a highly aggressive personality, one moreover who articulates a representative element in the society into which Pip has been born. Notice the combination of 'market economics' and violence! What Dickens presents to us on this occasion is a group of adults who, with the exception of Joe, are all linked by an expressly aggressive attitude towards Pip. Pumblechook is, in effect, a spokesman for the group, and 'insight' into his *individual* condition is beside the point.

Dickens is concerned to establish something general about Pip's world, shared in various degrees by almost all the adults he meets, certainly by Mrs Joe, and an instance of which he has already dramatically encountered in his churchyard meeting with the convict. The point is further underlined in the following chapter when Pip, watching the genuine conviviality that springs up between Pumblechook, the sergeant, and the rest while they are waiting for Joe to repair the handcuffs, thinks to himself:

> what terrible good sauce for a dinner my fugitive friend on the marshes was. They had not enjoyed themselves a quarter so much, before the entertainment was brightened with the excitement he furnished. (Chapter 5, p. 64)

Ratified, we may say, by the authority of the State (in the person of the sergeant going about the King's business) the company discover in the fugitive convict a more pleasurable target than Pip for their aggressive feelings. We notice too that Pip, who in the previous chapter felt deep guilt at his enforced connection with the convict, now calls him 'my fugitive friend'.

The characterization of Pumblechook is indeed 'of the surface' in a technical way, but far from being lacking in 'insight', it points directly to the kind of society Pip finds himself growing up in. We may think of it as Dickens's technique for presenting people in their social roles, and so a way of saying something about the society that allots its members such roles. The absence of inner self-consciousness in such characters is neither here nor there, because the method of characterization is directed to a different end.

Here is another example of 'surface' presentation, from Chapter 2:

> My sister, Mrs Joe, with black hair and eyes, had such a prevailing redness of skin that I sometimes used to wonder whether it was possible she washed herself with a nutmeg-grater instead of soap. She was tall and bony, and almost always wore a coarse apron, fastened over her figure with two loops, and having a square impregnable bib in front, that was stuck full of pins and needles. She made it a powerful merit in herself, and a strong reproach against Joe, that she wore this apron so much. Though I really see no reason why she should have worn it at all: or why, if she did wear it at all, she should not have taken it off, every day of her life. (p. 40)

This is our first impression of Mrs Joe. And while we gain further impressions from her behaviour towards both Pip and Joe, we never get direct access to her inner self-consciousness, nor to why she is as she is. Her actions are, on the whole, predictable, and her speech, if more varied than Pumblechook's, typically resorts to repetitious formulae, of which 'bringing Pip up by hand' becomes the most familiar. What is your view of the above paragraph? How does Dickens succeed in presenting Mrs Joe in terms of 'surface', which nevertheless tells us much of what we need to know?

DISCUSSION

The first sentence suggests, does it not, a kind of self-directed aggression? Admittedly, it is only Pip's fancy that she washed her face with a nutmeg-grater rather than soap, but the image remains with us, as not inconsistent with what we positively learn about her. The second sentence is unambiguous: 'a *square impregnable* bib in front, that was stuck full of pins and needles'. (We learn in a moment that, when cutting slices of bread for Joe and Pip, she holds the loaf against this bib so that pins and needles get into the slices.) What more succinct account of her resentment of the caring maternal role could we look for? Considered in the light of these details, we can then look back at the first four words of the paragraph: 'My sister, Mrs Joe'. No first name. Nor even 'Mrs Joe *Gargery*', in itself indicative as her relationship with Joe reveals. That relationship might indeed be thought one of the novel's enigmas. Is her violent personality of the kind that needs to provoke violence in others, so that Joe's deliberately pacific attitude towards her exacerbates rather than soothes? Her attitude towards Orlick, after he has clubbed her down, is submissive, even affectionate? (See Chapter 16, pp. 150–1.) Certainly, Dickens doesn't go into this relationship, which is to one side of his principal concern with 'Pip's Progress'. But what he does set out wholly in terms of the 'surface' method incorporates pertinent and subtle observations, sufficient to dispose of the view that the method as such is limited. A more complex example of Dickens's way of presenting his characters it to be found in Chapter 8, when Pip has his first sight of Miss Havisham. Here are the paragraphs in question.

> I entered, therefore, and found myself in a pretty large room, well lighted with wax candles. No glimpse of daylight was to be seen in it. It was a dressing-room, as I supposed from the furniture, though much of it was of forms and uses then quite unknown to me. But prominent in it was a draped table with a gilded looking-glass, and that I made out at first sight to be a fine lady's dressing-table.

Whether I should have made out this object so soon, if there had been no fine lady sitting at it, I cannot say. In an arm-chair, with an elbow resting on the table and her head leaning on that hand, sat the strangest lady I have ever seen, or shall ever see.

She was dressed in rich materials – satin, and lace, and silks – all of white. Her shoes were white. And she had a long white veil dependent from her hair, and she had bridal flower in her hair, but her hair was white. Some bright jewels sparkled on her neck and on her hands, and some other jewels lay sparkling on the table. Dresses, less splendid than the dress she wore, and half-packed trunks, were scattered about. She had not quite finished dressing, for she had but one shoe on – the other was on the table near her hand – her veil was but half arranged, her watch and chain were not put on, and some lace for her bosom lay with those trinkets, and with her handkerchief, and gloves, and some flowers, and a prayer-book, all confusedly heaped about the looking-glass.

It was not in the first few moments that I saw all these things, though I saw more of them in the first moments than might be supposed. But, I saw that everything within my view which ought to be white, had been white long ago, and had lost its lustre, and was faded and yellow. I saw that the bride within the bridal dress had withered like the dress, and like the flowers, and had no brightness left but the brightness of her sunken eyes. I saw that the dress had been put upon the rounded figure of a young woman, and that the figure upon which it now hung loose, had shrunk to skin and bone. Once, I had been taken to see some ghastly waxwork at the Fair, representing I know not what impossible personage lying in state. Once, I had been taken to one of our old marsh churches to see a skeleton in the ashes of a rich dress, that had been dug out of a vault under the church pavement. Now, waxwork and skeleton seemed to have dark eyes that moved and looked at me. I should have cried out, if I could. (p. 86–7)

There is, admittedly, some artificiality in abstracting these paragraphs from their context, preceded as they are by Pip's arrival in the strangely-named Satis House, and followed immediately by the account of how Miss Havisham behaves towards him and Estella. Nevertheless, read the extract again with these questions in mind: what elements in this 'surface' presentation of Miss Havisham direct us to the 'inner' truth, both about her and about her role in the novel? And why does Pip give us two separate accounts of what he saw?

DISCUSSION

Pip has already been established as both keenly observant and well able to convey memories of what he had observed. (If you haven't already registered this, glance again through Chapter 1 (e.g. the last three paragraphs, pp. 38–9) or the opening of Chapter 3, (p. 48).)

Here these earlier impressions about him are confirmed. He reports not just the obvious points (wedding dress, veil, bridal flowers, white hair), but also the evidence that the lady had not finished dressing (one shoe on, the other at hand, the veil half-arranged, the confusion of objects on the dressing table, the prayer-book). Notice that such details confine us to what the young Pip can *understand* of what he sees: their further significance (well-known to the narrator) is at this point withheld. The fixed position of the lady, elbow on table, head on hand, the half-disarray of her appearance, the prayer-book: all these are tell-tale signs of her whole story, which the reader learns only when Pip first meets Herbert (Chapter 22). But we surely discover a good deal about her? There is the third paragraph (cunningly introduced by Pip's disclaimer that doubtless he didn't see everything at first), which superimposes on the first description of Miss Havisham as (white hair apart), the young bride-to-be she had once seemed, a second description as she appears now: the dress yellow and faded, the flowers withered, and the wearer of the dress no longer showing the 'rounded figure of a young woman' but 'shrunk to skin and bone'. This trick of double exposure is a good example of the adult narrator interpolating, indirectly, impressions that his younger self could not have gathered. Pip could only have seen the aged Miss Havisham; the young Miss Havisham of the second paragraph not only could not have been observed by *anyone*, she could only have been imagined by someone who knew Miss Havisham's story.

Finally, there are the last three sentences. Pip had seen, on an earlier occasion, a skeleton, richly dressed, and a waxwork of some stately personage: 'Now waxwork and skeleton seemed to have dark eyes that moved and looked at me. I should have cried out, if I could.' Reading these sentences, we have travelled a long way from 'she was dressed in rich materials'. Our first impression of them might well be: 'we know Pip is fanciful; such details speak only of his understandable childish fears.' But in truth, the notion of a living skeleton is no more than a summary of Miss Havisham's psychological state, and of the deadly influence she brings to bear on Pip, and on Estella. Taken as a whole, these paragraphs summarize the key points about Miss Havisham's existence and her role in the novel – fixated on her past injury, revenging herself on the present. So if 'surface' characterization can suggest so much, it can hardly be thought a limited technique. Yet it is fair to add that, in the comparison with Pip's account of Mrs Joe, there is here a noticeable shift in method, represented in Pip's final comparison of Miss Havisham to skeleton and waxwork. Here we have, not 'surface' presentation, but imagistic comparisons, writing more 'poetic' than descriptive. It is a point about the language of *Great Expectations* that we'll discuss further.

Further examples of this method of presenting his characters can be found in the novel. You might like to consider for yourself: Jaggers (Chapter 11, pp. 111–2, Chapter 18, pp. 163ff.); Wemmick (Chapter 21, p. 195 and Chapter 24, pp. 221–4); and the Pocket family (Chapter 23).

One character however isn't presented to us in this way: Pip himself. As one would expect in an 'autobiography', his inner life is copiously accessible to us from the outset. So much is true, certainly, of the young Pip. But is it true of the adult narrator? We know from the last few pages of the novel that, now in his mid-thirties, Pip had become a modestly successful Victorian business-man working in the firm of his friend Herbert Pocket. But these are external formalities. What kind of man is he? Or is that an irrelevant question? What is your view on this point? What impressions have you gained of the character telling the story, and how have they arisen?

DISCUSSION

It seems to me that Dickens does present the adult narrator as 'a character' and for at least one prominent reason: the novel relates 'Pip's Progress'. *Great Expectations* shows (amongst other things) how the little boy we first meet in that opening encounter with Magwitch grew into the man who, in the last section of the novel, fully accepts the filial identity (at first bitterly unwelcome) that Magwitch came to impose upon him. In these opening chapters especially, I gain my impression of the man from two sources. There are the several explicit paragraphs of commentary on the behaviour of his younger self. For example, in Chapter 8:

> My sister's bringing up had made me sensitive. . . Within myself, I had sustained, from my babyhood, a perpetual conflict with injustice. I had known, from the time when I could speak, that my sister, in her capricious and violent coercion, was unjust to me. I had cherished a profound conviction that her bringing me up by hand, gave her no right to bring me up by jerks. Through all my punishments, disgraces, fasts and vigils, and other penitential performances, I had nursed this assurance; and to my communing so much with it, in a solitary and unprotected way, I in great part refer the fact that I was morally timid and very sensitive. (p. 92)

This is informative about Pip as a child, but even more so about the man he became: self-aware, analytic, sombre (yes?), with a note of resigned sadness.

Or again, meditating on the fact that he never confessed to Joe about the file he stole for Magwitch:

> In a word, I was too cowardly to do what I knew to be right, as I had been too cowardly to avoid doing what I knew to be wrong. I had had no intercourse with the world at that time, and I imitated none of its many inhabitants who act in this manner. Quite an untaught genius, I made the discovery of the line of action for myself. (Chapter 6, p. 72)

Our narrator is evidently a moralist, and a stern one. (Do *we* think the young Pip cowardly because he stole the food and file for the convict?) Then, there is the characteristic touch of ironic bitterness ('quite an untaught genius'). The novel shows many such comments which, collectively, suffuse it with a moral sensibility very much the narrator's.

Neither of these examples, though, properly represents another aspect of the narrator, which emerges less through direct commentary, than through his own narrative style, those occasions when his individual mixture of sympathy and detachment, sombreness and humour, emerge from the way he actually recounts the past. Here is a brief exercise to illustrate the point. Write out your own version of the second paragraph of the novel, concentrating on the basic facts which it communicates. Then ask yourself what is lacking in your account and evidently present in the novel.

DISCUSSION

It is not difficult to recount the principal facts about Pip and his parents that the paragraph sets out. But it surely is impossible to catch, except in the original words, the interplay of pathos and humour that arises from Pip's imagining what his parents actually looked like by gazing on the lettering of the tombstones. There is the phrase 'five little stone lozenges' (p. 35), a euphemism both comic and sad; the generalizing irony of 'gave up trying to get a living, exceedingly early in that universal struggle'; and the final childish fantasy about his five brothers having been 'born on their backs with their hands in their trouser-pockets.' The fanciful account rings entirely true of the young Pip, trying to puzzle out something about his family from this meagre evidence. The narrator re-tells these fancies, but within the different perspective of an adult's sense of the whole human situation: both parents and five infants, all dead, leaving Pip, and of course, his formidable sister. This complex narrative tone fully conveys the young Pip's isolation and vulnerability, while the touches of humour (if that *is* the word?) keep at bay sentimental appeals on the simple ground of his being an orphan. We are to be interested in Pip, as we soon discover, for different reasons than (in Dickens's day) on account of that altogether common state of affairs.

A final briefer example. Pip is on his way to the Battery with the food stolen from his home.

> The mist was heavier yet when I got out upon the marshes, so that instead of my running at everything, everything seemed to run at me. This was very disagreeable to a guilty mind. The gates and dykes and banks came bursting at me through the mist, as if they cried as plainly as could be, 'A boy with Somebody-else's pork pie! Stop him!' The cattle came upon me with like suddenness, staring out of their eyes, and steaming through their nostrils, 'Holloa, young thief!' One black ox, with a cravat on – who even had to my awakened conscience something of a clerical air – fixed me so obstinately with his eyes, and moved his blunt head round in such an accusatory manner as I moved round, that I blubbered out to him, 'I couldn't help it, sir! It wasn't for myself I took it!' Upon which he put down his head, blew a cloud of smoke out of his nose, and vanished with a kick-up of his hind-legs and a flourish of his tail. (Chapter 3, p. 48)

I leave you to decide what sentence or sentences represent the narrator's view of the occasion, as distinct from Pip's, which the paragraph mainly is intended to convey, and how that contributes to our sense of the narrator as a character.

There is one novelistic 'contraption' that we still need to consider: the narrative itself. We have discussed the teller of the tale, and his shifting relationship to it – sometimes overt through commentary, on other occasions no more than implicit, and on yet others wholly merged with that of his childhood self. But what *kind* of tale is it? And is its formal organization something we need to attend to? It seems to me that, as readers, it is not long before we sense that this is a novel with a 'strong' story-line, generating the kind of narrative momentum we particularly associate with detective novels and thrillers, where the question 'how will the story end?' dominates consciousness. In using the term 'story' in that last sentence, I am conscious that you may have wanted to say 'plot'. Novels in which the discovery of some previously hidden piece of information, a discovery that clears up all the tantalising uncertainties that have kept us reading in the expectation of just such a clarification and winding-up, are usually thought of as having an emphatic 'plot'. Most narratives have 'plot', though some (say, fairy tales, legends) have very little. Dickens, in general, goes in for 'plots', and in this sense at any rate, *Great Expectations* is typical. We'll come back to the difference between 'story' and 'plot',[6] but let us first look more closely at the first section of the novel for evidence of the particular structure needed to give the reader a sense of 'plot'. Glance over the first ten chapters, and make a note of details, actual episodes or comments on them, which hint at the 'plot' of *Great Expectations*.

DISCUSSION

Different readers will, of course, come up with different reactions, but here is mine. The first six chapters pitch us into a helter-skelter sequence of events, beginning with Pip's encounter with the convict in the graveyard, ending with his capture and Pip's return home. We learn nothing about what this will mean in Pip's later life, save only that he accuses himself of moral cowardice for not telling Joe the whole story, that it was he, and not Magwitch, who stole the food, drink and file (Chapter 6). Magwitch has suddenly invaded Pip's existence – and then as suddenly disappeared from it; why, we do not know. Nor do we know why Magwitch, having escaped from the Hulks, instead of getting away altogether, chooses to ensure that the other escaped convict (about whose identity we are told nothing) was recaptured. So it is only in the next group of chapters, telling of Pip's first visit to Satis House, that I first notice clear signs of the 'plot' of *Great Expectations*. Chapter 8 closes with Pip's painful realization that, from Estella's point of view, he was just 'a common labouring-boy' (p. 94), with coarse hands, too-thick boots, and pitifully ignorant about the right name for knaves; in other words, with that first shaming onset of the 'class-consciousness' that will dog his subsequent life. Then, in Chapter 9, reflecting on his day at Satis House, Pip comments:

> That was a memorable day for me, for it made great changes in me. But, it is the same with any life. Imagine one selected day struck out of it, and think how different its course would have been. Pause you who read this, and think for a moment of the long chain of iron or gold, of thorns or flowers, that would never have bound you, but for the formation of the first link on one memorable day. (p. 101)

Here is the narrator in his role as moralist inviting readers to confirm a general truth. The metaphor of the chain, together with the sombre advice to ponder the course of our own lives ('pause you who read this') underlines for us that Pip's encounter with Miss Havisham and Estella is the first in a sequence of events that will shape his life for good and/or ill. Notice that the language both reveals and conceals at once. Is Pip's chain to be of iron, or of gold? (Do we remember here the iron chains used to shackle the captured convicts?) Is it to be made of flowers, or of thorns? The ambiguity here is entirely characteristic of those narrative signs, or clues, which novelists deploy in the service of a 'plot', and from now on, we are surely on the look-out for further signs that will answer the question: what *kind* of chain, whose first link is represented by Satis House, will bind together the events of Pip's life? We soon find out that his experiences there fire him with the ambition to become a 'gentleman', an ambition that makes us a major part of the 'plot' of the novel, but whether this constitutes a golden or an iron chain remains long in doubt.

The second episode that signals the 'plot' of the novel seems to me to follow in the next chapter. Pip has been told by Mrs Joe that on his way home from school he should collect Joe from the village pub, The Three Jolly Bargemen. There he finds the stranger who looks at him with special keenness, asks about his name, his relation to Joe, the lonely church on the marshes, and having bought some drinks all round, carefully stirs his with an iron file:

> He did this so that nobody but I saw the file; and when he had done it, he wiped the file and put it in his breast-pocket. I knew it to be Joe's file, and I knew that he knew my convict, the moment I saw the instrument. I sat gazing at him, spell-bound. (Chapter 10, p. 106)

The mysterious stranger's gift of a shilling wrapped in two grubby pound-notes gives Pip no pleasure. The pound-notes, stored away in the parlour by Mrs Joe remain for Pip a nightmarish reminder of his secret 'conspiracy with convicts – a feature in my low career that I had previously forgotten' (pp. 107–8). What could constitute a clearer sign for the reader that the meeting with Magwitch, supposedly a thing of the past, an inexplicable irregularity that has no real connection with Pip's normal life, is nothing of the kind? Magwitch is still present in Pip's life – if only by proxy. The evidence of a linked sequence of events, the kind that we call a 'plot', is unambiguous. Yet it's also more mysterious than the paragraph noting Pip's thoughts about the Satis House visit. That paragraph tells us there is a 'plot' unfolding. The meeting with the stranger in the pub only hints at the possibility of one. Notice, here, that the incident belongs with the group in which the adult narrator simply withholds information from the reader, identifying himself wholly with young Pip. Only in Chapter 39, with Magwitch's return to London, do we understand the point of the meeting with the mysterious stranger. Dickens is nevertheless careful to keep the presence of this hidden 'Magwitch-plot' alive. As an exercise, you might go through the remaining chapters of this first section of the novel, and note how this is contrived.

Nevertheless it is the 'Havisham-plot' that provides the main substance of these chapters, described by Pip, as we have seen, as initiating a set of events in his life that resembles a golden or iron chain. A question to ask then is: does the reader share Pip's notion that the secretive benefactor, whose plans for Pip Mr Jaggers announces in Chapter 18, is indeed Miss Havisham? What clues are we given, one way or the other? Are we confined to Pip's level of insight and understanding, or are we offered a different view? And whichever way you have decided, is this a merely 'formal' question about the narrative, or does more depend upon it?

DISCUSSION

Again, different readers will come up with different impressions. Also, it's not always easy to disentangle one's initial thoughts about a novel read for the first time, from those that derive from a second reading. My own view is that we are very largely confined to Pip's consciousness in his relationships with Miss Havisham. To take an example: when Pip visits her in his brand-new gentleman's clothing just before he departs for London (Chapter 19), there is no evidence that Miss Havisham is actively encouraging *him* in illusion, though that is certainly what she succeeds in doing. She enters into his prospects with something like enthusiasm.

> 'Ay, ay!' said she, looking at the discomfited and envious Sarah with delight. 'I have seen Mr Jaggers. *I* have heard about it, Pip. So, you go tomorrow?'
>
> 'Yes, Miss Havisham.'
>
> 'And you are adopted by a rich person?'
>
> 'Yes, Miss Havisham.'
>
> 'Not named?'
>
> 'No, Miss Havisham.'
>
> 'And Mr Jaggers is your guardian?'
>
> 'Yes, Miss Havisham.'
>
> She quite gloated on these questions and answers, so keen was her enjoyment of Sarah Pocket's jealous display. (p. 184)

How could Pip guess at the trick she is playing? And how could we? We do know that Miss Havisham delights in tormenting her fawning relatives. But we are unlikely to suppose that she here fosters the notion that she is Pip's benefactress simply to make Sarah Pocket jealous. On the other hand, the scene is bracketed by two revealing descriptions of Miss Havisham. When he arrives, she remarks on his appearance:

> 'This is a gay figure, Pip,' said she, making her crutch play around me, as if she, the fairy godmother who had changed me, were bestowing the finishing gift. (p. 183)

Do you notice the ambiguity in that 'as if'? On the one hand, it introduces a picturesque account of the scene; on the other, it represents Pip's illusion that she *is* the fairy godmother. Then, as Pip leaves:

> She stretched out her hand, and I bent down on my knee and put it to my lips. I had not considered how I should take leave of her; it came naturally to me at the moment, to do this. She looked at Sarah Pocket with triumph in her weird eyes, and so I left my fairy godmother, with both hands on her crutch stick, standing in the midst of the dimly lighted room beside the rotten bride-cake that was hidden in cobwebs. (p. 184)

The 'as if' has disappeared: she now is '*my* fairy godmother'. We then meet the sinister image that follows. . .

I find this episode characteristic of the handling of Pip's relationship with Miss Havisham. By and large, we are confined to his sense of the situation. The crucially coincidental role of Jaggers in both the plots (Havisham, Magwitch) is as hidden from us as from everybody else in the tale. Mrs Joe and Pumblechook are convinced that Miss Havisham will 'do something' for Pip, and Miss Havisham seems eccentric enough to be capable of adopting a poor country lad in order to spite her relatives. But then, on the other hand, when she paid Joe the money for Pip's apprenticeship, she explicitly said that ended the matter. We have had the hints about Magwitch's continuing interest in Pip. And we have the interpolated comments of the narrator which, collectively, hint at surprises to come. Why else the prominence of his criticisms of his younger self? In these ways Dickens lays the groundwork for a different interpretation of events than the one Pip reaches, though hardly one that the acutest reader could at first guess.

Did you decide that this point *was* merely 'formal', so that when we grasp the nature of the game Dickens is playing with his readers, beyond noting his skill in giving and withholding clues, there is nothing to add? Or do you sense a further significance? My own view is that there is more to be said, the point at issue being the degree of Pip's responsibility for his error. Was he a victim of a cruel prank? Or was he self-deluded? As you know, he directs no blame against Miss Havisham and appears to accept her verdict ('You made your own snares. *I* never made them.' Chapter 44, p. 374). But do we accept that verdict? That seems to me the substantial issue engaged by the development of the 'Havisham-plot' in these early chapters.

At the beginning of this chapter, I suggested that the tripartite division of the novel, coupled with the explicit marking of 'stages' in the unfolding of Pip's expectations, appear to shape the tale as a kind of 'progress'. Would you now read over Chapter 19 for other suggestions of this kind? Note especially the last paragraph, where there is an allusion to the end of *Paradise Lost*, when Adam and Eve leave the Garden of Eden.

> Some natural tears they dropped, but wiped them soon;
> The world was all before them, where to choose
> Their place of rest, and Providence their Guide.
> (Book XII, ll. 645–7)

Given the differences of situation, how might this allusion direct us to think about Pip at this point?

DISCUSSION

What strikes me about the presentation of Pip in this chapter is the speed with which his new expectations damage his relationships with Joe and Biddy. Of Joe, he is at once ashamed (or rather, perhaps we should say, many earlier such thoughts now surface). He envisages schemes for 'improving' Joe's life, raising him from his humble uneducated-blacksmith's state. With Biddy, long the sharer of his inmost hopes and dreams, he is insufferably patronising: 'I am extremely sorry to see this in you, Biddy. . . It's a – it's a bad side of human nature' (p. 176), he loftily retorts when she objects to such plans for Joe. He equally resents her implied criticisms, and makes his resentment felt. In a word, Pip appears in the most unfavourable light: snobbish, ungrateful, condescending, even cold. We sense the adult narrator's implicit presence very strongly in such scenes, judging his younger self as thoroughly contemptible.

Pip's Progress', then, seems unlikely to be a case of simple congratuation. (His most assiduous admirer is now *Pumblechook* – surely a sign of trouble-to-come?). In that light, the allusion to the end of *Paradise Lost* is interesting. Adam and Eve leave Paradise because of their fall from innocence to live out the common human condition Shakespeare has in mind when he says 'The web of our life is of a mingled yarn, good and ill together' (*All's Well That Ends Well,* IV, iii, 83). The sentence 'the mists had all solemnly risen now, and the world lay spread before me' (p. 188) follows immediately on Pip's account of how he *kept meaning* to leave the stage-coach, go back home, and make 'a better parting' – but didn't actually do so. Pip enters on the 'second stage of his expectations', the narrator implies, having fallen from 'innocence' by a kind of primal betrayal of Joe, his sole protector and comforter in the days when Mrs Joe brought him up by hand. We touch here, surely, the source of the narrator's critical view of the boyhood he has been recounting.

3. Thematic

In the previous chapter, we concentrated on key 'formal' aspects of *Great Expectations*, using Chapters 1–19 in illustration. As we go on to discuss later chapters, try to keep these 'formal' issues in mind: the shifting role of the narrator; the interplay of the two plot-lines; the ambiguous or enigmatic clues that keep us, as readers, looking for the solution to the puzzles; and further the sense in which Pip himself gradually takes on the role of detective, the uncoverer of 'plots', seeking to unravel the complex of long past events that have impinged upon his life.

In this chapter, we turn to 'themes'. From being observers and analysts of the novel's 'contraptions', we become interpreters, makers of patterns that yield 'meaning'. We begin to ask: what is the novel *about*? And in pursuing this line, we need to remember that just as 'plots' and 'characters' are selections and abstractions from the complex verbal texture of the novel, the same is true of 'themes'. To search for 'themes', is to be *determined* to 'make sense' of the mass of detail, to arrange what seems casual or accidental into coherent relationships, and thus resolve the ambiguities and contradictions into a unified pattern. As a preliminary exercise here is a paragraph from an essay on *Great Expectations* setting out the writer's main analysis (which the essay proceeds to elaborate in detail):

> The story of Pip falls into three phases which clearly display a dialectic progression. We see the boy first in his natural condition in the country, responding and acting instinctively and therefore virtuously. The second stage of his career involves a negation of child-like simplicity; Pip acquires his 'expectations', renounces his origins, and moves to the city. He rises in society, but since he acts through calculation rather than through instinctive charity, his moral values deteriorate as his social graces improve. This middle phase of his career culminates in a sudden fall, the beginning of a redemptive suffering which is dramatically concluded by an attack of brain fever leading to a long coma . . . In the final stage of growth he returns to his birthplace, abandons his false expectations, accepts the limitations of his condition, and achieves a partial synthesis of the virtue of his innocent youth and the melancholy insight of his later experience.[1]

As an 'interpretation' of the novel, how does this impress you? Any significant omissions? Wrong emphases? Inaccuracies? Given that only so much can be said in one paragraph, does this seem broadly right or broadly wrong? Is it on the right lines, but over-neat? The point of these questions is to prompt you to your own overall act of interpretation – whether this takes the form of assent to, some qualification, or outright rejection of this account. Don't forget that each of these views would require supporting 'evidence', that is to say, reference to episodes in the novel that support your case. You might usefully make brief notes to this effect at this point, on at least one of the novel's three parts.

DISCUSSION

Here is my response to Stange's account. First, inaccuracies. There's more to the first phase of Pip's life than simple, instinctive virtue: false social values affect him from the time of his first visit to Satis House, and he gets food for Magwitch as much out of fear as kindness. In the second 'city' phase, his relations with Wemmick and Herbert show that, despite his 'gentlemanly' attitudes, he's still capable of disinterested acts; and though ashamed of Joe, he does nothing so dramatic as renounce contact with him. In the third phase, he abandons his false values *before* he returns to his home, mainly as a consequence of Magwitch's return to London, and the change this brings about in Pip. Next, omissions: Stange's virtuous-country/vicious-city contrast ignores the fact that Mrs Joe and Pumblechook are, in their own way, quite as keen on social advancement as the Pocket family, to say nothing of the influence of Satis House (the symbol of such values) in Pip's home environment. More striking is the absence in Stange's account of the presence throughout the novel of the adult narrator. The three-part structure of the novel is important, as we've noticed, but it is heavily qualified by the ubiquitous presence in all three parts of the narrator's personality, introducing into the whole novel the state of mind that Stange describes as the result of the third part. Generally, I think this account, though useful in noting the clear three-part structure, is over-neat, though the point would take to much space to justify here. Briefly – its neatness edits out Pip's hopeless love affair with Estella (this we are never allowed to forget) as well as Pip's complex, fanciful, elusive state of mind, both of which contribute to the story a haunting, suggestive, and 'poetic' quality which seems to me central to its interest.

A further reason for this discussion of Stange's view is to bring home the point that in interpreting novels we are necessarily involved in debates with other interpreters. Once a novel has become widely known, and widely studied, it follows that there will be many readers, and so many interpreters, at whatever level of tenacity and expertise. Interpretation is by no means the be-all and end-all of literary study, but it has its place, and an important function of this *Guide* is to encourage you to enter in your own terms into the interpretative debate.

Pressing the question, then: what is the 'theme' of *Great Expectations*? What is it *about*? Here is one kind of answer:

> *Great Expectations* is about an orphan called Pip, harshly brought up by an elder sister, but on affectionate terms with her blacksmith husband. One winter day Pip accidentally meets an escaped convict, and is kind to him. The convict is later recaptured. In the following winter Pip meets a rich eccentric spinster with a pretty niece, who live in a nearby town. They make him feel ashamed of his humble origins. Some years later he is apprenticed to the blacksmith's trade, but he dreams of becoming a gentleman and marrying the pretty niece. . .

Reliable enough in its way? But all it really adds up to is the re-telling of Dicken's story in condensed form – and less interesting language. It doesn't get at the 'theme', or 'subject' of the novel, because it fails to grapple with the problem of the story's relation to 'life'. If we ask, in this sense, what *Great Expectations* is about, the answer would have to take this form:

> *Great Expectations* is about an unhappy love affair, or about the cost of false social expectations, or about the connections between crime and riches. . .

I list these as alternatives, but of course they don't exclude each other, and you may want to add – or substitute – others. It's rarely possible to sum up in a phrase or two what any substantial novel is about. We should think of 'themes' rather than 'theme', 'subjects' rather than 'subject'. One reason why you can have more than one acceptable interpretation of a novel is that, while critics may broadly agree that such-and-such themes are dealt with, there's always room for argument about which comes first. (You've already had an example of such argument in my comments on Stange's view. For him, the way Pip grows up through three different phases is what matters, whereas I put more stress on the finished adult telling his own story, and thereby exploring his own nature.)

One way of identifying a novel's themes is to look for the clues that writers always provide. Another way is to follow the principle some critics call 'the figure in the carpet' (from the title of a story by Henry James, referring to the partly hidden design that gave order to the rich confusion of detail in the carpet). We look, that is, for a pattern that makes sense of the details of the story. Arguments between commentators characteristically turn on this question of what does constitute an inclusive pattern. So, it's always a reliable first 'move' in interpretation, even in those cases where the novelist supplies plenty of overt clues, because there will still be areas of the work where you are left on your own.

This is certainly the case with *Great Expectations*. We have seen that it takes the form of a pseudo-autobiography in which the adult narrator both tells the story of his past life, as it was actually experienced, and directs the reader to an interpretation of this story by interpolated commentary. Does this commentary offer us an overview of what Pip's story amounts to? Up to a point. But, here we have to recall that this commentator, or interpreter, is the adult Pip, and like all the other characters in the story, is a 'fiction'. *His* interpretations of his past life are, in the last analysis, fictional details that in themselves require interpretation. The 'figure in the carpet' offered us by the adult Pip is no more than a prominent element in the design that, as readers, it remains our task to construct.

So what do we begin by looking for, above and beyond the hints and directions offered by the *Great Expectations* narrator? 'Figures in the carpet', which is to say, patterns, are established by means of recurrences and repetitions. Let me suggest one such pattern, which perhaps you've already noticed in the early chapters: education. Do you recall any details in the story that would support the proposal that 'education' is a theme of the novel?

DISCUSSION

It depends, doesn't it, on how 'education' is to be defined? Taken in the sense of 'schooling', certainly there is some evidence that Dickens wants us to consider the poverty of educational provision for such as Pip: his early schooling in the village, if schooling it can be called; Joe's illiteracy; and Pip's determination to get such learning as he can, the help he gets from Biddy. We can add to that Pip's further education under the tutelage of Mr Pocket. Pip draws our attention to its importance by noting that, despite his extravagant and empty London existence 'through good and evil I stuck to my books' (Chapter 25, p. 227). We might even add to this list Magwitch's lack of any education at all. But is this enough to establish 'education', in that sense, as a 'theme'?[2] I would prefer to argue for a broader definition of the term, the whole process of equipping children for adult life. We could then see Pip's young life as the product of mis-education. Mrs Joe not only gives him no help, but actively discourages any sign of intelligence as certain to lead to the Hulks (Chapter 2, p. 46). Joe can only help in limited ways, though these are significant nonetheless. Miss Havisham exerts a malign influence over both Pip and Estella, and Pumblechook's bullying arithmetic 'games' amount to a parody of what helpful teaching might be. Magwitch intends well, yet his narrow conception of a 'brought-up gentleman' is shown as stultifying. Indeed, Magwitch's own early life can be included in the 'theme'. Pip asks:

> 'What were you brought up to be?'
>
> 'A warmint, dear boy.'
>
> He answered quite seriously, and used the word as if it denoted some profession. (Chapter 40, p. 345)

The full account of Magwitch's childhood is directly relevant here (see Chapter 42, pp. 361*ff*.)

Education, so defined, necessarily covers what we would describe today as social attitudes, so that discussion of an educational theme in the novel inevitably widens into this broader issue. Let us call it the 'social theme'. I've suggested earlier that the way Dickens presents the characters of the story points to the kind of society these characters inhabit. There is some risk of banality in making this point. As a *genre*, the Novel's outstanding feature is its ability to represent man-in-society more fully and intensively than other kinds of writing. One reason for this derives from the range of characterization that novels make possible, a development, incidentally, to which Dickens made an impressive and influential contribution. This can be seen at once in *Great Expectations*, despite its primary focus on Pip, because of the range of people whom he comes into contact with: Miss Havisham, and the Pocket family; her tenant, the thriving tradesman Pumblechook, and other local worthies of the town, including Trabb's boy; her legal adviser, Jaggers, his clerk Wemmick, and the shadowy criminal types who haunt Little Britain; the village blacksmith, Joe, and his journeyman, Orlick; soldiers, convicts, notably Magwitch, and of course, the 'gentlemanly' convict Compeyson. These characters can be further grouped into the respectable and the criminal, Pip having a foot in both camps, thus raising to explicitness the relationships that exist between the two. Jaggers, in a different way, also belongs in both camps, making his living out of crime, and not altogether respectable himself: he terrifies the magistrates (Chapter 24, p. 225), his servant is a murderess, and he relishes potentially violent types such as Bentley Drummle (Chapter 26, p. 234).

We need then to define 'social theme' more exactly. How would you do this, and what aspects of the story would you point to? (Remember the point about recurrence.)

DISCUSSION

The first 'clue' in helping to define the 'social theme' more exactly seems to me to lie in Pip's comment following his first visit to Satis House (Chapter 8):

> . . . I set off on the four-mile walk to our forge; pondering, as I went along, on all I had seen, and deeply revolving that I was a common labouring-boy; that my hands were coarse; that my boots were thick; that I had fallen into a despicable habit of calling knaves Jacks; that I was much more ignorant than I had considered myself last night, and generally that I was in a low-lived bad way. (p. 94)

There are many later examples: his adolescent dreams of becoming a gentleman; treatment of Biddy and Joe; bad influence on Herbert's finances; pointless festivities with the Finches of the Grove; first reaction to the discovery that Magwitch is the source of his wealth; and so on. We reach one aspect of this theme through the adult Pip's self-critical comments on his social aspirations as a young man. It is the narrator's tone of voice, above all, that directs us how to think of this: disgusted with the self that he was; angry at the influences that affected him; resignedly ironic about the power of trivial social detail ('calling knaves Jacks'); and often, I think, despondent at the damage done – to himself, as well as others.

Did you notice any other evidence? I'd suggest these. A lot of the comic detail reinforces Pip's view of the social issue: Pumblechook's farcical servility; Trabb's boy's splendid take-off – 'don't know yah, pon my soul, don't know yah!' (p. 267); Mrs Pocket's feeling that she'd married beneath her; Herbert's satisfaction in marrying a girl without parental encumbrance. These incidents also show that the influences working on Pip permeate the whole society. His story may be unique in its detail, but it also has a *typical* quality, embodying social forces that affect everybody in one way or another. As the various incidents accumulate, we begin to sense the wide – and destructive – power of 'gentlemanly' aspirations. Finally, too, there is Magwitch's history. The main part of his sufferings was at the hands of a 'gentleman', and a legal system strongly influenced by 'gentlemanly' appearance. Perhaps the most vivid indictment stems from the effect of Magwitch's plans for Pip, generously intended but ruined by the convict's determination to create a gentleman of his own to flaunt in the face of society. In a sense, Magwitch's money damages Pip more grievously than does Miss Havisham, because it enables him to pursue an arid social goal.

You will see that I have assumed – not very originally – that the 'social theme' *is* the idea of becoming a 'gentleman'. The evidence is, of course, not just the central role of Pip in the novel, but the amount of the rest of it that this theme makes sense of. But there are other aspects to the theme, which we'll come back to.

Meanwhile, here is another critic's comment on the issue.

> Dickens was attempting to define within the middle classes some such boundary as he had already accepted between the respectable and the low. In the last resort he shared Magwitch's belief that money and education can make a 'gentleman', that birth and tradition count for little or nothing in the formation of style. The final wonder of *Great Expectations* is that in spite of all Pip's neglect of Joe and coldness towards Biddy and all the remorse and self-recrimination that they caused him, he is made to appear at the end of it all a really better person than he was at the beginning. It is a remarkable achievement to have kept the reader's sympathy throughout a snob's progress. The book is the clearest artistic triumph of the Victorian bourgeoisie on its own special ground. The expectations lose their greatness, and Pip is saved from the grosser

> dangers of wealth; but by the end he has gained a wider and deeper knowledge of life, he is less rough, better spoken, better read, better mannered; he has friends as various as Herbert Pocket, Jaggers, and Wemmick; he has earned in his business abroad enough to pay his debts, he has become a third partner in a firm that 'had a good name, and worked for its profits, and did very well'. Who is to say that these are not advantages? Certainly not Dickens.[3]

What do you think of that as an account of the novel? Make a note of points you agree with, and points you disagree with.

DISCUSSION

Here is my list of agreements/disagreements.

(a) A 'snob's progress' exaggerates: Pip becomes a bit snobbish, but this is never more than an aspect of his 'progress'.
(b) I don't share this critic's difficulty in sympathizing with Pip's development.
(c) I agree that Dickens approves the fact that Pip becomes a hard-working Victorian business man. (The 'gentleman' Compeyson didn't do this, but took to fortune-hunting and crime; Herbert, despite his Pocket origins, proves himself by hard work.)
(d) Whether the novel shows us that Dickens thought 'money and education' can make a gentleman, I am less certain. But it is true that Pip makes his transition from blacksmith's apprentice to man-about-town with the minimum of difficulty.

However, House's comment was not cited just for the sake of arguing with it. It is surely useful in clarifying Dickens's case against 'gentlemen'. It wasn't the possession of money he was attacking, nor being well educated (remember how Pip stuck to his books), nor the respectable middle-class life which Herbert and his wife doubtless enjoyed. Hence House's emphasis on the novel as an expression of the Victorian bourgeoisie, the class to which Dickens himself belonged, and – by and large – was pleased to belong. What, precisely, is the criticism of the 'gentleman' idea? I think the answer is quite straightforward: 'gentlemen' don't work. They live on inherited money, or on 'expectations', leading a life of leisured dissipation, running up extravagant debts which they get out of if they can. Pip's life as a Finch of the Grove is in this tradition: for example, his influence on Herbert – Pip and his friends are bowdlerized versions of the Regency rake, wining, dining and womanizing – see Calder's note on the reference to Covent Garden,

(Chapter 34, p. 292). There is a pattern of hostile references in Dickens's novels to life in this style, and an opposing approval of the virtues of hard work and the gains of honest effort. Pip's experience is Dickens's most extended attack on the issue, but other elements in the novel contribute to the same effect: Compeyson in one way, Herbert in another. Satis House itself represents the sterility of 'gentlemanly' leisure. The disused brewery was once a place of thriving, productive energy, but not now. Partly this can be read as a symbol of Miss Havisham's life-hating vengeance, but it also shows more directly Dickens's view of a style of leisured life cut off from the work that, economically, it depends on.

In the article we've already touched on, Robert Stange makes the interesting further point that as well as attacking one conception of a 'gentleman' the novel suggests a positive alternative, the kind of honourable, self-forgetful person Pip turns into.[4]

This is worth emphasizing because it reminds us that the concept 'gentleman' is not simple. The *Oxford English Dictionary* lists a range of usage, including:

Sense 3 A man of chivalrous instincts and fine feelings.

Sense 4 A man of superior position in society; often, a man of money and leisure.

Stange, in effect, suggests that 'Pip's Progress' represents his development from Sense 4 to Sense 3, and we could note that the same opposition is represented in the contrast between Mr Pocket and Herbert on the one hand, and Compeyson and Bentley Drummle, on the other. Whether, though, Dickens really develops a 'fictional' exploration of these two kinds of gentlemanliness is questionable. There is this revealing exchange between Pip and Herbert which makes no reference to the issue.

> 'You call me a lucky fellow. Of course, I am. I was a blacksmith's boy but yesterday; I am – what shall I say I am – today?
>
> 'Say a good fellow, if you want a phrase,' returned Herbert, smiling, and clapping his hand on the back of mine, 'a good fellow, with impetuosity and hesitation, boldness and diffidence, action and dreaming, curiously mixed in him.' (Chapter 30, p. 269)

Is it that Herbert is being 'gentlemanly' in the good sense by tactfully evading the social implication of Pip's question? Or is it that Dickens, writing in the mid-Victorian period, would rely on his readers to supply what is not here stated: that Pip is no longer a blacksmith's boy, but has yet to prove himself a gentleman of the stamp of Herbert? We'll look at this point again later. Meantime, I hope you'll agree that the subject *is* important to the novel as a whole, and sufficiently recurrent in one context after another to constitute a principal theme.

But is that all there is to the 'social theme'? Let us pursue the question further, from a different direction, by taking up another point raised in House's comment.

If you shared anything of my reaction, you'll have found very odd his idea that Dickens pulled off a great artistic triumph simply by keeping us sympathetically interested in such an unattractive person as the young Pip. But suppose House is right, how did Dickens manage it? Or, if you prefer, how would you explain to a critic such as House that you had no difficulty in remaining sympathetic towards Pip? Here are some possible reasons:

(a) We sympathize with Pip because Dickens shows him to be a victim of society who cannot be blamed for his mistakes.
(b) the autobiographical form of the novel in itself aligns our sympathies with Pip, and makes it very difficult to dislike him.
(c) The severe view of Pip really comes from his adult self looking back on his youthful blunders. We are not meant to adopt this view as our own.
(d) The centre of the novel is the adult Pip whom we like and admire precisely because he doesn't disguise or try to excuse the unattractive actions of his youth.

List these reasons in the order of their effectiveness in persuading a critic like House to sympathize with Pip.

DISCUSSION

You may have found it hard to decide on the ranking. They're all valid points: reason (b) is the least persuasive argument because, despite the autobiographical presentation, Dickens clearly wants us to disapprove of Pip on account of some of his actions. Reason (a) is a half-truth, which we'll come back to in a minute. Dickens shows that strong pressures are working on Pip, but to call him a 'victim' does him less than justice. Reason (d) seems to me unarguable. But perhaps it doesn't occur to us till after we've finished reading, so I may be overrating its persuasive force. (House's point centres on how we feel about Pip as we read.) Finally, I think reason (c) needs only small qualification to counter House's argument. We are not meant to disagree with the adult Pip's severe criticisms of his younger self, but to remember the powerfully mitigating circumstances Dickens puts before us.

You may be wondering what the connection is between that exercise and further exploration of the 'social theme'. Are questions about our view of Pip, and how the narrative 'structure' affects it, a digression from issues of 'theme'? On the contrary, what I wanted to bring out was that you can't deal satisfactorily with 'theme' except in relation to the fictional 'structure'. However much time you spend on looking for supporting detail, your interpretation will be vulnerable if it doesn't reflect an adequate grasp of the 'structure'.

House's comment shows this well. His point that Dickens underwrites Pip's Victorian middle-class values is perceptive, but, misreading the 'structure', he takes the 'theme' to be 'a snob's progress', and defines the novel as 'the clearest artistic triumph of the Victorian bourgeoisie on its own special ground' – meaning, I suppose, that it clearly affirms the qualities separating a moderately prosperous, well-educated and hard-working Victorian bourgeois from, on the one hand, the parasitical lower reaches of the leisured aristocracy and, on the other, the grossly servile, thoroughly hard-hearted commercialism of Pumblechook. It seems, at best, a limiting judgement! What makes Pip's experience so much more than 'a snob's progress' is the presentation of his story through the mind of the adult narrator, and it is from this fictional 'structure' that the 'social theme' emerges.

I called it a half-truth to view Pip as 'a victim of society who cannot be blamed for his mistakes'. Did you agree with this? It is certain enough that the course of Pip's life is substantially determined by the two key events that we learn about in the first section of the novel, which initiate the 'plots' emanating from Miss Havisham's actions and from Magwitch's. On the other hand, in relating these events the adult Pip nowhere suggests that, as a consequence, he is to be viewed as a 'victim'. On the contrary, as we've seen, his criticisms are mainly directed at his younger self. We recognize, for instance, that the violence and injustice of Mrs Joe's behaviour are certainly to be blamed, but the story doesn't imply for a moment that responsibility for the way things turn out for Pip is to be shifted from his shoulders to hers. The stress falls again and again on Pip's mistakes in judgement, on his failure in loyalty to such as Joe. But are the narrator's judgements to be endorsed by the reader? I've already suggested that, like everything else in the novel, they too require interpretation. We can perhaps check on this by considering whether other characters are implicitly judged in the same way – that whatever the social pressures, they remain responsible for their actions. Can you think now of appropriate examples?

DISCUSSION

Consider the presentation of Mrs Havisham. Her cruel treatment of Estella and Pip follows from her betrayal at the hands of Compeyson. More subtly, the obsessive ritual in the blighted wedding-room reveals the self-punishing character of her life. (You could even think of Pip and Estella as ruined versions of the children she might have had.) Yet in coming to understand Miss Havisham, do we exactly 'forgive' her as Pip does? Not, at any rate, in the sense of thinking her any the less responsible for what she did. Dickens shows how much she, personally, chooses the sterile pattern of her own life, the tragically pointless revenge which hurts nobody but two children, and herself. The explanation of her conduct certainly doesn't explain anything away.

Other examples support this view. Compeyson and Orlick are presented, without explanation or excuse, as unredeemably villainous. Joe and Biddy are presented as straightforwardly good. Joe, we could easily imagine behaving very differently towards Mrs Joe and, as if to anticipate such a reaction, Dickens has Joe explain to Pip just why he is so forbearing: he remembers how his violent father treated his mother (Chapter 7, pp. 76–7). But that doesn't detract from our sense that Joe deserves the approval that Dickens clearly wants us to give him. And as to Pip, there is evidence that Dickens did want readers to endorse his own sense of keen self-blame. In his notes about the end of the novel (which you will find printed in an Appendix to the Penguin edition), Dickens wrote:

> So goes abroad to Herbert (happily married to Clara Barley), and becomes his clerk.
>
> The one good thing he did in his prosperity, the only thing that endures and bears good fruit. (p. 495)

So, in his last conversation with Miss Havisham, Pip insists that it is he who needs 'forgiveness and direction' (Chapter 49, p. 410.) Here, if anywhere, is a point where Dickens might have suggested Pip was overdoing his self-accusations. The adult narrator, for example, might have remarked that this was the natural overreaction of a young man who'd been taking his first hard look at his own life. But there is nothing of the kind. All the signs are that we are to think Pip's attitude perfectly in order.

Are we then to conclude that the 'victim of society' angle is entirely wrong? If it is, then, in effect, we must agree with House's view of Pip's life, based as it seems to be on the express view of the narrator that he behaved shamefully towards Joe and Biddy. Yet it is precisely in some of the narrator's comments that we find the most explicit statements that Pip was a victim of his life shaped by the effects of other people's scheming. We've already noticed one of these comments (see p. 101) as the first explicit sign to the reader of the 'Havisham-plot', Pip's remark about a chain of iron or gold binding together certain events in his life. He makes another such remark in the chapter which precedes Magwitch's arrival at his rooms in London.

> And now that I have given the one chapter to the theme [his love for Estella] that so filled my heart, and so often made it ache and ache again, I pass on, unhindered, to the event that had impended over me longer yet; the event that had begun to be prepared for, before I knew that the world held Estella, and in the days when her baby intelligence was receiving its first distortions from Miss Havisham's wasting hands. (Chapter 38, p. 330)

And he goes on to compare his situation with that of the victims of the sultan who, by long and secret plotting, arranged for a stone slab to fall upon them: 'So, in my case; all the work, near and afar, that tended to the end, had been accomplished; and in an instant the blow was struck, and the roof of my stronghold dropped upon me.' The chain of events culminating in Magwitch's return to London was begun by Compeyson, Miss Havisham and her half-brother, Jaggers and Magwitch, long before Pip was born. The notion of a great stone, dropping in predetermined fashion upon the fragile structure of his hopes is hardly an exaggeration.

I would want to argue then that, depending on the choice of evidence, Pip is presented (he presents himself!) *both* as responsible for the course of his life, *and* as a mere pawn in the schemes of others, for which he has no responsibility whatever. The scales are loaded so evenly, and the issue is so central to the novel, that I believe it needs further exploration. Here are some paragraphs from an essay that directly addresses the problem:

> Pip is framed as a victim, an unconscious victim deceived by accident and intention, impelled into a position of maximum exposure to destruction and saved only because, as Dickens believed . . . there is reason to have faith in human nature inasmuch as it contains in itself compensatory powers, inherent impulses towards spiritual regeneration . . .
>
> [in the novel] life is shown as a dangerous enterprise where we must make decisions without being able to foresee their outcome or consequences and where intention or will go for nothing . . . Dickens shows, in spite of our having to live blindfolded, and in spite of being

> handicapped by nature and fettered by the social condition, we *can* achieve contentment and self-respect if not happiness. This is what Pip is shown as winning his way to in the face of apparent total disaster. . .
>
> We thus grasp . . . that the narrator is now truly a free man, freed from the compulsions of childhood guilt and from shame imposed by the class distinctions that closed around him in his boyhood, and from the unreal aspirations imposed on him by his society – a society from which when he grasps its true nature he is finally seen to recoil. Yet we have also seen that the guilt and shame were necessary to produce the complex sensibility of an adult who can free himself by renunciation, contrition, and publicly manifested repentance. This is Pip's history . . .[5]

These brief extracts contain the gist of the essay. It is the young Pip who is the victim, confused and overborne by the cultural and social pressures represented by Mrs Joe, Miss Havisham, Estella and Magwitch. The moral judgements proceed from the adult Pip who has freed himself from these influences, and can now tell his story with mature self-knowledge. The point of the novel is to show *how the young Pip became the adult narrator*, a man who has sufficient self-knowledge to tell his own story clearly, and who has gained this self-knowledge by learning to act against the false values which had invaded his youth, and to rebuild his life round true relationships and real attainments.

Re-read the extracts from Mrs Leavis's essay. What events might she choose which show the young Pip making the kind of moral decision which directs his life into sounder channels than those dug for it by early social influences? List three, if possible.

DISCUSSION

I would choose, (a) his decision to help Magwitch, despite feelings of intense social and moral revulsion; (b) his refusal to blame Miss Havisham; (c) his earlier decision – secretly – to help Herbert with his career.

All these events show Pip acting, not in terms of social aspiration, or hopeless love, but from a sense of what he thinks is right. In different ways, they mark his progress away from living a 'gentlemanly' life on 'great expectations', towards the hard-working clerk who pays his debts and finally returns to enjoy the domestic scene of the final chapter. There are other events that illustrate this side of Pip, but I think these are the most striking.

Mrs Leavis's analysis has in its favour one point that I've already stressed. She puts the adult Pip at the centre of the novel (contrast House, who sees only the child and young man), and I think some such recognition of the narrative structure necessary to any sound interpretation. An equally good point is the connection she finds between Pip's personal development and the movement and interaction of the two 'plots' which, as noticed in Chapter 1, provide the key to the narrative structure.

Magwitch's return is the surprise that throws new light on everything that precedes it, and accounts for the direction of everything that follows. Dickens referred to this event when he spoke of 'the grotesque tragi-comic conception' of his story (see p. 2). All the ambiguities of the early part of the story, all those cunningly introduced details which leave the reader wondering whether or not Pip *is* deluded about Miss Havisham, are now seen in a true light. We now recognize, perhaps for the first time, the total futility of Pip's passion for Estella. And the same event controls all the remaining story. What is Pip to do with Magwitch? What is he to do with himself? These questions, occurring to us almost as soon as to Pip, lead straight to the final chapters. What Mrs Leavis's account brings out is *the connection between this sequence of events and their meaning for Pip*. Magwitch's return provides him, she argues, with the most severe imaginable test. It is not only that he has to face the loss of Estella, and of the promised 'gentleman's' life. He recognizes that Magwitch must be looked after, and that *he* must do it. It's easy for the reader to think only of the pathos of Magwitch's behaviour, to forget that from Pip's point of view he's a threateningly unattractive figure, socially and morally. Would it have been altogether surprising if Pip had repudiated him? (The far less embarrassing Joe makes him intensely uncomfortable.) Or worse, might he not have drifted into patronizing him for the sake of his money? It's when Pip decides to stick to Magwitch, taking no advantages, no 'portable property', for himself, that the would-be 'gentleman' peels away, leaving a man of courage, sensitivity and humane feeling. Mrs Leavis argues that the plot turns on this event because it is also the point at which Pip-the-victim begins his strenuous climb towards the self-responsible maturity of the adult narrator, free of the damaging social pressures of his youth. In this way, both the narrative method and the movement of the plot combine to express the subject of the novel: 'in spite of being handicapped by nature and fettered by the social condition, we *can* achieve contentment and self-respect if not happiness. This is what Pip is shown as winning his way to in the face of apparent total disaster. . .'[6]

I find this a persuasive argument, yet it depends heavily on our accepting that there is a clearly delineated character whom we know as 'the adult Pip'. Is this the case? We have seen in Chapter 2 that, as narrator, Pip does convey a distinctive personality, mainly by way of his comments on events. But apart from that, isn't he a rather shadowy figure? What kind of concrete social existence can we envisage for him at the end of the novel? It's noticeable that the eleven years that have passed since he joined Herbert's firm were spent *abroad*, and in the final pages, he is a *revenant*, visitor to a place where he no longer *has* a place. Nor should we forget that, in telling his tale, he displays quite remarkable narrative skill which nevertheless we do not really credit to him, but to the novelist. Could it be that the adult Pip is no more than a necessary 'fiction' through whom the real novelist, Charles Dickens, chooses to organize the novel?

Let me suggest a different view of 'the adult Pip', by following once again a basic rule that should guide interpretation. We've already seen, in discussing the theme of 'gentlemanliness' that it appears not only in Pip's history, but in many other contexts. In that sense, then, Pip is socially *typical*. Might there not be equal typicality in the presentation of Pip both as morally responsible and the product of the powerful social forces variously represented in the two 'plots'? Where else in the novel do you find that double perspective on characters and events?

DISCUSSION

Magwitch's account of his life is surely the outstanding case.

> This is the way it was, that when I was a ragged little creetur as much to be pitied as ever I see. . . I got the name of being hardened. "This is a terrible hardened one," they says to prison wisitors, picking out me. "May be said to live in jails, this boy." Then they looked at me, and I looked at them, and they measured my head, some on 'em – they had better a measured my stomach – and others on 'em giv me tracts what I couldn't read, and made me speeches what I couldn't unnerstand. They always went on agen me about the Devil. But what the Devil was I to do? I must put something into my stomach, mustn't I? (Chapter 42, p. 361)

It seems to me, incidentally, that one of the great things about the novel is the timing of Magwitch's story immediately after his appearance in Pip's life as a tough, hardened, menacing ex-convict. It lays open the social context of Magwitch's whole life. Only now do you understand that mysteriously savage fight with Compeyson in the marshes. Dickens never calls Magwitch a 'victim of society', but when you remember his first name, the term is hard to avoid: Abel (in the Old Testament) was the brother and guiltless victim of the aggressive Cain.

On the other hand, there's no suggestion that he isn't as responsible as everybody else for the conduct of his own life. Indeed, he explicitly accepts that responsibility when he says 'Wotever I done, is worked out and paid for,' (Chapter 41, p. 360). The secret 'plot' connection between Pip and Magwitch can thus be seen to depend upon a real affinity between their situations, and that Pip eventually becomes a sort of son to Magwitch has its appropriateness.

For other characters presented in the double perspective (both morally responsible human beings, yet also scarred by social determinants) we could turn to Jaggers and Wemmick. Neither lacks human feelings, yet both are shaped (misshaped?) by the harsh presssures of money and work in an inhumane legal system. Both cultivate an outward professional hardness, a strictly commercial attitude to experience. Wemmick lives a double life, a second Jaggers in Little Britain, a devoted and affectionate son in his home. Jaggers seems more completely professional, his home life correspondingly grimmer. His rescue of Estella from the wretched life she might have had is our only definite evidence of kindly feelings. Perhaps they still persist. He seems to have a sort of affection for Pip. On the other hand, there's the memorable scene when he forces his housekeeper, Estella's mother, to show her scars, and there's his ominous satisfaction in the bullying, morose Bentley Drummle.

And we might even want to add to the list Miss Havisham who, in some degree, is presented as a product of a specific social condition, yet also as morally reprehensible.

So, it does seem that the novel offers other examples of the predicament primarily experienced by Pip, and this to me suggests an explanation for the relatively elusive condition of his final 'adult' state. As a boy and a young man, his life allows Dickens to present a memorably typical figure who embodies the contradictions inherent in the society depicted in the novel. Whereas, as fully-formed adult narrator, such experiences now belonging to his past, he is primarily a fictional device, a novelistic 'contraption' for opening up the nature of the society embodied in his own early history. The connection between this adult narrator and his past self is left vague as being to one side of Dickens's primary preoccupation with the social context. Who better than Pip as narrator to convey the waste and damage in his own life brought about by that context? That task fulfilled, his adult existence is not important to Dickens.

Having now put my own 'thematic' cards on the table, let me stress again that the point of these discussions about 'theme' is not primarily to persuade you to *agree*, but rather to exercise and develop your own interpretive skill and insight. The best way to find out whether you do agree with any of the views I have presented is to begin by disagreeing, and then elaborating an argument that assembles different aspects of the novel which these views have ignored, or reassembles the same aspects in a new way. And as to agreement, don't forget that in this kind of discussion, simply nodding your head isn't enough: you also need to take hold of the idea, and make it your own by pursuing its further consequences.

4. Realism and Language

In Chapter 2, we concentrated on formal aspects of *Great Expectations*, beginning from the question: how far does Dickens want us to be conscious that a novel is what we are reading? The answer I suggested was: it depends on the particular episode. Sometimes, the narrator withdraws his commenting presence, and also his overall knowledge of events, to bring us as closely as possible to the young Pip's experiences. Sometimes, he makes us entirely conscious that he is telling us a story, from which he has drawn certain conclusions about life. Yet, after a while, since it is his own story, and Dickens presents Pip as directly addressing his readers, we begin to take these comments as an element in *his* experience, and forget that it is just 'a story'. Here and there we also sense the presence of the novelist's overall shaping purpose, as when he mentions 'stages' in Pip's progress, but on the whole, the very procedure of first-person narration is a means of persuading us that the story is 'real', that we are looking through it, as through a window, into events in the world. On the whole, then, becoming conscious of the novel as a 'fiction' requires a particular effort of analysis, and if we don't make that effort, as Chapter 3 proposes, we make little progress in grasping the novel's theme(s): what it has to say about 'life'.

A more general term for Dickens's novel, in these respects, would be to say that it adopts the conventions of nineteenth-century 'realism'. It offers to draw the reader into a 'fiction' that is nevertheless sufficiently like the 'real world' to convince us that it is. Why is it necessary to say this? Does it seem a mere academic game of classification necessary in an account of literary history but having no bearing on our reading experience? An important reason for claiming that it is relevant to that experience has been proposed in the critical discussion of novels in recent decades. To forget that 'realism' is a particular fictional technique is to ignore the pre-eminent role of language in novels.[1] As I have suggested, such concepts as 'character', 'plot' and 'theme' refer only to particular arrangements and sequences of the words in which any novel is written. If, for example, there were no proper names supplied in the dialogue of *Great Expectations* we would have no way of relating speeches to speakers, yet a proper name is simply another *word* (admittedly, of a special kind). A 'character' in a novel is, in the end, a group of sentences and paragraphs of description, physical and psychological, which are first attached to a particular proper name, so that when that name recurs we are able to understand a summarizing reference to those sentences and paragraphs. It is, we may say, a verbal mimicry of real human behaviour, and what is at issue is a question about the status of such mimicry, or 'imitation', to use the more dignified critical term. How far do novels 'imitate' real life, and how far do they impose upon it illusory and escapist substitutes? We are accustomed to expecting novels to present us with satisfactory conclusions, by which we usually mean a solution to the problems and predicaments the story has set out. But isn't this altogether *unrealistic*? How many of the problems and predicaments of real life – moral, social, political – are solved and brought to a harmonious conclusion? The novelistic resolutions brought about at the end of a novel are, in effect, solely verbal. The fact that we expect and take pleasure in them doesn't in the least make them 'real', if we mean by that, having a direct correspondence with events in the world.[2] In this chapter, then, let us look more closely intertwined issues of 'realism' and of the language of

Great Expectations as a way of bringing home the degree to which, like all novels, it is composed of words in much the way that a piece of music is composed of sounds, and a painting of pigments.

We can engage the 'realism' issue at one level by considering a prominent aspect of the two 'plots' of the novel. In the second section (Chapters 20–39) how does Dickens keep alive the enigmatic presence of the 'Magwitch-plot' throughout a series of chapters dominated by 'Havisham-plot' in the shape of Pip's conviction that she is his benefactor, and by her encouragement of his hopeless love for Estella? You could look especially at Chapters 28, 29, and 32 for relevant detail.

DISCUSSION

I suggest that there are two rather different methods. One is the pattern of coincidences that continue to link Pip with the criminal underworld. When he first journeys from his home village to Little Britain, where Jaggers has his legal offices, the first place he visits is Newgate Prison; his meeting with Jaggers is repeatedly interrupted by the latter's clients (Chapter 20), and later with Wemmick he visits Newgate Prison (Chapter 23). Returning for a visit to Miss Havisham he finds himself travelling with two convicts under arrest who are conversing about the two pound-notes Magwitch had sent Pip by the hand of the mysterious stranger (Chapter 10). Pip hears an actual reference to Magwitch when the convict, whom he recognizes as the stranger, says to his companion that he'd been asked to 'find out that boy that had fed him [i.e. Magwitch] . . . and give him them two one pound notes' (Chapter 28, p. 251). How, as first-time readers, do we take such episodes? Probably we don't see the significance of his contact with criminal life via Jaggers because, like Pip, we know only of Jaggers's formal connection with Miss Havisham. Pip's accidental encounter with the convict of the pound notes may perhaps strike us differently. Do we write it off as accident, and therefore as 'real' – the persuasive role of much casual and contingent detail in novels? Or do we notice the specific reference to the episode in Chapter 9, and to Magwitch, and think further about them?

Perhaps again, with Pip, we write it off as an accident whose point is to bring home how much he is still guiltily affected by the memory of his childhood episode. But there is a second set of incidents to account for. In the next chapter, Pip goes to Satis House and there meets Estella for the first time since boyhood. They stroll round the old brewery and Pip reminds her of her contemptuous treatment of him in the old days. Watching her closely, he imagines a fleeting resemblance between her and somebody else. But who? This happens four times. The third and fourth as reported like this:

> As my eyes followed her white hand, again the same dim suggestion that I could not possibly grasp, crossed me. My involuntary start occasioned her to lay her hand upon my arm. Instantly the ghost passed once more, and was gone.
>
> What *was* it? (Chapter 29, p. 259)

Notice the typographical prominence of that last sentence. It happens that Jaggers is also visiting Satis House, so Pip takes the chance to ask whether Estella's second name is indeed *Havisham*, or some other name, and Jaggers confirms that it is Havisham. Here, surely, the reader is being signalled to notice a mystery about Estella, though it is equally true that the signal remains obscure. Three chapters on, the signal is more pronounced. When Pip is about to meet Estella in London on her way from Satis House to Richmond, he happens first to be conducted round Newgate Prison by Wemmick. Then, waiting for Estella's coach, he ponders on his continued association with 'this taint of prison and crime', remembers his meeting with Magwitch, feels abhorrence at the contrast between such ideas and Estella, and wishes he could shake off 'the soiling consciousness of Mr Wemmick's conservatory' on this day of all days. The coach arrives and he sees Estella's face at the window. Whereupon the chapter ends with this sentence.

> What *was* the nameless shadow which again in that one instant had passed? (Chapter 32, p. 284)

What indeed? To whom is this question addressed? Why does Pip suddenly adopt this somewhat 'stagey' language? The actual wording, as indeed the visual separation of the question from the preceding paragraph, gives it a special resonance. As with the meeting with the mysterious stranger in Chapter 9, this unanswered question makes us sense the presence of 'plot', even if we can't take it further than that. Only on a second reading do we grasp what has been at stake with these encounters with Estella: Pip has glimpsed that resemblance between her and her mother, Jaggers' housekeeper, and perhaps too with her father Magwitch, which will eventually lead him to the truth about her parentage. Far from being in a wholly different world than that of 'prison and crime', Estella is a daughter of that world. The connection between them is the opposite of casual; it rather points to an underlying truth.

What has this to do with the issue of 'realism'? Simply, that the felt presence of 'plot', brought about here by elements of managed coincidences, prompts in more or less degree a recognition of the fictional status of the episodes. Moreover, Dickens must want us to recognize this because it is the means whereby he expresses a central theme of the novel, the role of impersonal social pressures in shaping individual lives. Notice that there is a certain paradox involved. Dickens wants the pattern of coincidences to be sufficiently unremarked by the reader to prevent it from contradicting the overriding 'realistic' convention of the novel, working to disguise its own novelistic procedures and to create a convincing illusion of 'real life'. Yet if the reader altogether fails to notice the pattern, then Dickens's preoccupation with the way society shapes individual lives will not be communicated.

The device of 'coincidence' is, in fact, a characteristic Dickensian way of establishing narrative pattern, and as we've seen in Chapter 3, pattern is the key in the search for 'themes'. In the case of the two 'plots', the pattern could be further described as one of hidden resemblance: sequences of events that *seemed* to have no connection turn out to point to a shared meaning. That apparently casual 'realistic' link between Pip's visit to Newgate and the arrival of Estella is revealed – in fact, partly declares itself, though still obscurely – as 'fictional': the novelist's purposive shaping of the narrative in such a way as to connect Pip to Estella by means of their relationships with Magwitch. Such episodes may not at first seem a product of specific items of 'language'. It is a feature of narrative 'realism' to adopt a language that seems transparent, a language we don't notice *as language* because it adopts the grammar and constructions we use for reporting actual events. But *Great Expectations* makes extensive use of a different kind of writing where a failure to notice *language as language* will mean that we don't take in what Dickens is wishing to convey. We have already considered a case in point: Pip's first sight of Miss Havisham in Satis House (Chapter 8). You might now glance again at the discussion of the description he reports (see pp. 28). Then read in Chapter 11 the description of the room in Satis House which contains the ruined wedding-feast. What do you notice about descriptions of this kind, and of the writing that conveys them to us?

DISCUSSION

The first account of Miss Havisham's appearance concludes with a style of writing that we can reasonably think of as 'poetic'. It uses imagery, metaphor, analogies, comparisons, rather than statements, and on inspection we notice a certain rhythmical structure.

> Once, I had been taken to see some ghastly Waxwork at the Fair, representing I know not what impossible personage lying in state. Once, I had been taken to one of our old marsh churches to see a skeleton in the ashes of a rich dress, that had been dug out of a vault under the church pavement. Now, waxwork and skeleton seemed to have dark eyes that moved and looked at me. I should have cried out, if I could. (p. 87)

Do you see how the sinister effect of the penultimate sentence, implicitly comparing Miss Havisham to a waxwork and a skeleton 'in a rich dress', greatly depends upon the preceding two sentences, which show a common rhythm and syntactical structure ('Once I had been taken . . . Once I had been taken. . .')? So too the 'double exposure' effect already discussed, whereby the description of Miss Havisham as a young bride is overlaid by that of her withered state, derives from carefully selected *changes* in detail (white, then yellow, etc.) Then, when we turn to the description of the ruined wedding-feast, we find a further description of death and decay, summed up by Miss Havisham's statement that when she died, her corpse would be laid out on the table where the cake stood.

In describing such writing as 'poetic' in some degree, I am not suggesting any failure of immediate 'realism'. On the contrary. Yet, it is clear, I think, that these descriptions, together with the haunted sterility of Satis House as a whole (the empty brewery, the neglected garden), come to represent for us Miss Havisham's morbid and diseased state of mind and feeling. This is what the descriptions stand for, or, to use the more technical term, 'symbolize'. And it is a general point about the language of the novel that episodes and descriptions, which at first present themselves within the 'realistic' mode, can be subtly transformed in the direction of 'symbol': they point, that is, beyond their immediate meaning within the linear progress of the story, to some further more complex, though also often elusive, meaning.

We can make a rough-and-ready analogy with changes in camera focus and position in cinema or television. We're all familiar with the fact that when the 'shot' changes from a wide-angle survey of a scene and zooms into a close-up on some item or person within it, we are expected to attach a special significance to the object or person. Shifts in the character of narrative language work in much this way, though less obtrusively and on the whole with greater subtlety.

'. . . that the dark flat wilderness beyond the churchyard, intersected with dykes and mounds and gates . . . was the marshes; and that the low leaden line beyond, was the river; and that the distant savage lair from which the wind was rushing, was the sea . . .' (Chapter 1, pp. 35–6)

For another example, please read Chapter 25, the account of Pip's first visit to Wemmick's home in Walworth. Wemmick's Castle and grounds are described in some detail. Is this a diversion from the main story? What is Dickens getting at here? How do these pages contribute to the main story? Does the description seem 'realistic', or not?

DISCUSSION

Looked at from the angle of Pip's story, his visit to Wemmick (Chapter 25) has some importance. It begins a friendship between Pip and Wemmick necessary to the dénouement, when Wemmick helps Pip in the arrangements for Magwitch's escape. But that hardly accounts for the extraordinary character of Wemmick's domestic arrangements, the tiny wooden cottage described as a Castle, the drawbridge, the flagstaff, the nightly firing of the Stinger, the pigs, poultry and cucumber bed ('if you can suppose the little place besieged, it would hold out a devil of a time in point of provisions', p. 229), and so on. What is the point of all this? An amusing diversion from the main business of the novel? A mere exercise in comic fancy which the reader is expected to enjoy and forget about? Such an explanation fails to take account of two points. One is Wemmick's appeal to Pip to say nothing about Walworth to Jaggers.

> No; the office is one thing, and private life is another. When I go into the office, I leave the Castle behind me, and when I come into the Castle, I leave the office behind me. If it's not in any way disagreeable to you, you'll oblige me by doing the same. I don't wish it professionally spoken about. (p. 231)

The other is the striking division in Wemmick's personality between the affectionate and thoughtful son of 'the aged Parent', the attentive host to Pip (he cleans Pip's shoes) on the one hand; and on the other, the hard-faced lawyer's clerk who decorates his person with the various rings and other gifts from clients awaiting execution, and who models his professional 'office' behaviour on that of the formidably unsentimental Jaggers. Dickens makes quite sure we don't miss the point by the way he ends the chapter. As Wemmick and Pip walk back next morning to Little Britain, where Jaggers has his office, Wemmick changes:

> By degrees, Wemmick got dryer and harder as we went along, and his mouth tightened into a post-office again. At last, when we got to his place of business and he pulled out his key from his coat-collar, he looked as unconscious of his Walworth property as if the Castle

> and the drawbridge and the arbour and the lake and the fountain and the Aged, had all been blown into space together by the last discharge of the Stinger. (p. 232)

You'll remember that Wemmick's post-office mouth is one of the prominent details which Pip mentions on the occasion of their first meeting (Chapter 21). Even when Wemmick eats his lunch, this detail is underlined: 'Wemmick was at his desk, lunching – and crunching – on a dry hard biscuit; pieces of which he threw from time to time into his slit of a mouth, as if he were posting them' (p. 221). Yet this is the same man who grows his own cucumber salad, and makes sure that Pip 'tips' his deaf old father a nod, to make him feel properly attended to by the visitor.

We have, then, surely to see a 'symbolic' aspect to Wemmick's house. Indeed, the whole episode is an excellent example of Dickens's practice in inter-weaving the 'realistic' and the 'symbolic'. On the basic definition of 'realism' much detail is straightforward, presenting itself to the reader 'as if it were really happening', disguising the fact that we are reading a novel about entirely imaginary events. But the fantastic quality involved in the account of Wemmick's little estate signals a move towards 'symbol'. The method, however, doesn't altogether resemble the method adopted for Miss Havisham. It resides in the element of comedy, in the touches of subdued satire, that penetrate the description. Indeed, Pip's attitude to much of his visit to the Castle is ironic, though of course he is not so rude as to betray this to Wemmick.

> Then, he conducted me to a bower about a dozen yards off, but which was approached by such ingenious twists of path that it took quite a long time to get at; and in this retreat our glasses were already set forth. Our punch was cooling in an ornamental lake, on whose margin the bower was raised. This piece of water (with an island in the middle which might have been the salad for supper) was of a circular form, and he had constructed a fountain in it, which, when you set a little mill going and took a cork out of a pipe, played to that powerful extent that it made the back of your hand quite wet. (pp. 229–30)

The absurdity of these contrivances is not heavily underlined. But we are expected to notice it. Similarly implicit is the significance of the fact that when the Stinger is fired it 'shook the crazy little box of a cottage as if it must fall to pieces' (p. 231). We can surely read into this the fragility of the whole domestic structure within which Wemmick is able to express kindly feelings; even (if you want to push the analysis a bit further) the fragility of his own psychological solution to the problem of keeping some humanity intact while having to make his living in the harsh and cruel world of Little Britain. Dickens's method of alerting the reader to these deeper implications lies in this use of comic or satiric fantasy, rather than the 'poetic' language used to describe Miss Havisham's room. Yet the comedy is *also* an effect of language: the little fountain 'played to that powerful extent that it made the back of your hand quite wet'. The irony arises from the juxtaposition of 'powerful extent' followed at once by the evidence of the tiny dimensions of the fountain. Here, as in other respects, Dickens's text requires careful reading. You could perhaps now read again the account of Pip's visit to the Castle, and make a note of other such touches, that combine to remind the reader of how shaky the whole structure is in comparison with the solid and irremoveable Little Britain, Newgate, and Jaggers' sombre Soho house, the world of the criminal and criminal lawyer, upon which Wemmick's amiable domesticity finally depends.

Another aspect of the novel's language that is more 'poetic' than 'realist' is the recurrence of imagistic writing whose effect is to connect episodes and characters in unexpected ways. Attention to imagery in novels was encouraged by the study of poetry, especially of Imagist poetry of the early twentieth-century written on the principle that poets communicated less through ideas, arguments, or abstractions, than through clear visual images. We've already looked at the waxwork-skeleton image for Miss Havisham. But there are examples of imagery in *Great Expectations* less immediately striking, yet collectively as significant, primarily because the same or similar images unexpectedly recur in different contexts. For example, when Pip, and Joe have seen Magwitch hunted down and captured by the soldiers, he is taken back to the Hulks by a crew of other convicts.

> No one seemed surprised to see him, or interested in seeing him, or glad to see him, or sorry to see him, or spoke a word, except that somebody in the boat growled as if to dogs, 'Give way, you!' which was the signal for the dip of the oars. By the light of the torches, we saw the black Hulk lying out a little way from the mud of the shore, like a wicked Noah's ark. Cribbed and barred and moored by massive rusty chains, the prison-ship seemed in my young eyes to be ironed like the prisoners. We saw the boat go alongside, and we saw him taken up into the side and disappear. Then, the ends of the torches were flung hissing into the water, and went out, as if it were all over with him. (Chapter 5, p. 71)

The first sentences in this paragraph show the repetition of syntax and resulting rhythm that usually goes with writing in the 'poetic mode'. The Hulk is '*like* a wicked Noah's ark' and '*seemed* . . . to be ironed' like the prisoners, while the extinguishing of the torches has the effect of a death. But it is the detail 'growled *as if to dogs*' that I want to concentrate on. Earlier in the chapter, Magwitch and Compeyson, are called by the sergeant 'two wild beasts' (p. 67). Earlier still, in Chapter 3, Magwitch says to Pip, who has brought him the food, that he would be 'but a fierce young hound indeed' if he'd happened to have brought anyone else with him to capture Magwitch. Pip then describes Magwitch's eating in this way:

> I had often watched a large dog of ours eating his food; and I now noticed a decided similarity between the dog's way of eating, and the man's. The man took strong sharp sudden bites, just like the dog. He swallowed, or rather snapped up, every mouthful, too soon and too fast ... In all of which particulars he was very like the dog. (pp. 50–1)

These repeated comparison of Magwitch to a dog (or beast), and the tentative connection that Pip makes between Magwitch and a fierce hound accumulate a clear implication surely? The legal and social structure (remember that the sergeant is on the King's business) is revealed as dehumanising, both for hunted and hunters. Against this, Pip's action in giving Magwitch the food, as to a fellow-human being, and saying 'I am glad you enjoy it' (p. 50) represents a different quality of relationship, something we know Magwitch responded to and, in his own way, lived up to in respect of his plans for Pip.

Now turn to Chapter 8, and read the account of Estella's treatment of Pip after Miss Havisham has sent him away. What do you notice about it?

DISCUSSION

The context is Pip's first discovery of social shame. His coarse hands, and thick boots have led Estella to call him 'a stupid, clumsy labouring-boy' (p. 90). Estella treats him with cold contempt, and when she brings him his meal:

> She put the mug down on the stones of the yard, and gave me the bread and meat without looking at me, as insolently as if I were a dog in disgrace. (p. 92)

In itself, the comparison doesn't stand out. But if we think back to those earlier uses of 'dog', at least two implications present themselves. Pip and Magwitch are linked by a tenuous thread of verbal association, both treated as 'dogs'. There is no need at this stage of our discussion of the novel to labour the appropriateness of that link. The second implication is that the legal system that reduces that Magwitch, indeed all the convicts, to a dog-like condition has its analogy in the social system, the powerful combination of money and privilege and style we call 'class-prejudice', that encourages Estella to treat Pip as if he were a dog. And that this social system has the enthusiastic support of Pumblechook (which we learn on several occasions) is further reflected by his Christmas dinner invitation to Pip to consider his fate had he been born as a young pig. These details of language, then, already point to the broad structural equivalence of the Havisham and Magwitch plots, which will only be fully revealed in the last third of the novel. The general point to take from this example is that the figurative, metaphorical and more or less poetic writing that can be found on most pages of *Great Expectations* rewards careful attention.

look at the first paragraph of Chapter 8, describing Pumblechook's shop, and work out the effect of the language, and its broader significance for the story.

In his essay on the novel, Robert Stange argues for a pattern of images connected with stars and fires.

> Conflicting values in Pip's life are also expressed by the opposed imagery of stars and fire. Estella is by name a star, and through the novel stars are conceived as pitiless: 'And then I looked at the stars, and considered how awful it would be for a man to turn his face up to them as he froze to death, and see no help or pity in all the glittering multitude.' (Chapter 7, p. 80.) Estella and her light are described as coming down the dark passage of Satis House 'like a star', and when she has become a woman she is constantly surrounded by the bright glitter of jewelry. Joe Gargery, on the other hand, is associated with the warm fire of the hearth or forge. It was his habit to sit and rake the fire between the lower bars of the kitchen grate, and his workday was spent at the forge.[3]

You will find further examples of this pattern in Chapter 2, p. 41, and Chapter 34, pp. 291–2. Now consider whether the following belongs to the stars/fire pattern:

> I saw (Estella) pass among the extinguished fires, and ascend some light iron stairs, and go out by a gallery high overhead, as if she were going out into the sky. (Chapter 8, p. 93)

DISCUSSION

The stars/fire opposition does seem to be present, as it were, by implication. Estella, cold and unemotional, passes among the 'extinguished fires' of the disused brewery, where no work now goes on. (Whereas Joe's fire is an element in his work and his home.) Estella also appears as if 'she were going out into the sky', the place where stars become visible. Still, with a border-line example such as this, it's reasonable to hesitate. Just how much of the meaning of a complex work of literature a writer fully intends is a classic question for debate amongst critics. Yet we don't need to think of the sentence quoted above as prompted by deliberate, conscious reference to a pattern of star/fire images. But to relate it to the pattern does, I think, help to explain its poetic power.

In contrast, what is to be made of this paragraph?

> It was pleasant and quiet, out there with the sails on the river passing beyond the earthwork, and sometimes, when the tide was low, looking as if they belonged to sunken ships that were still sailing on at the bottom of the water. Whenever I watched the vessels standing out to sea with their white sails spread, I somehow thought of Miss Havisham and Estella; and whenever the light struck aslant, afar off, upon a cloud or sail or green hill-side or water-line, it was just the same – Miss Havisham and Estella and the strange house and the strange life appeared to have something to do with everything that was picturesque. (Chapter 15, p. 137)

DISCUSSION

Whether or not it belongs to a pattern of images, it suggests another view of Estella's meaning for Pip. It seems quite possible to argue that the sentence about Estella 'going out into the sky' links up with the paragraph above to suggest a different image for Estella – not the pitiless coldness of stars, but the sense of freedom, of aspiration, connected with enlarged horizons. Miss Havisham's connection with the paragraph is also problematic, because she's usually connected with everything artificial, and deathly. We might want to say here that Satis House, for all its deadliness in one respect, offers Pip a focus for his aspirations. Or should we remember that the place is the Battery where Pip gave Magwitch food, and that it is Magwitch who enables Pip to realize his aspirations? The immediate point to notice is that we shouldn't let prominent image patterns impose their meaning on the novel, but rather ask how they relate with other elements. By and large, Estella is the merciless star towards Pip, but the image in this paragraph registers something else as well. Indeed, we can go a bit further, and say that there's often ambiguity about image patterns. They don't necessarily mean one thing, or even two or three mutually consistent things. It's not always possible to say with complete confidence what they mean, though it's always worth asking.[4]

We have already seen that the language of the novel is the

source of comic effects, and Dickens's own emphasis on the tragicomic idea at the centre of the story underlines the role of comedy, often of a painful variety, in 'Pip's Progress'. One critic, John Carey, has even proposed that in the creation of his comic characters, Dickens has taken a sort of revenge upon his own sentimental side, and that his comic writing is invariably more lively and inventive, sharper in definition, less prone to a certain spurious rhetoric apt to emerge in the more sentimental stretches of his novels.[5] Certainly, *Great Expectations* is rich in comic interest. There is the near-farcical domestic comedy of Joe as the hen-pecked husband, being beaten and scolded by Mrs Joe; the satirical comedy that clusters round the pompous Pumblechook (the name itself does a good deal, as is the way with Dickens's names) and even touches Pip himself in the episode of Trabb's boy's imitation of Pip's grand ways; or the gentler comedy of manners generated by Joe's unsophisticated ways.

There is also a recurrent comic tone established by effects of language that are peculiarly 'Dickensian'. We've noticed this already in the discussion of Wemmick's house (see above pp. 62–3). Here is another example, illustrating a characteristic trait of Dickens's writing: a juxtaposition of the comic and the gloomy, even the horrific. Pip is describing his first London lodgings in Barnard's Inn:

> We entered this haven through a wicket-gate, and were disgorged by an introductory passage into a melancholy little square that looked to me like a flat burying-ground. I thought it had the most dismal trees in it, and the most dismal sparrows, and the most dismal cats, and the most dismal houses (in number half a dozen or so), that I had ever seen. I thought the windows of the sets of chambers into which those houses were divided, were in every stage of dilapidated blind and curtain, crippled flower-pot, cracked glass, dusty decay, and miserable makeshift; while To Let To Let To Let, glared at me from empty rooms, as if no new wretches ever came there, and the vengeance of the soul of Barnard were being slowly appeased by the gradual suicide of the present occupants and their unholy interment under the gravel. A frouzy mourning of soot and smoke attired this forlorn creation of Barnard, and it had strewn ashes on its head, and was undergoing penance and humiliation as a mere dust-hole. Thus far my sense of sight; while dry rot and wet rot and all the silent rots that rot in neglected roof and cellar – rot of rat and mouse and bug and coaching-stables near at hand besides – addressed themselves faintly to my sense of smell, and moaned, 'Try Barnard's Mixture.' (Chapter 21, pp. 196–7)

The predominant effect is of gloom and dirt, which communicates the subjective response of the young Pip. But the bizarre notion of the 'vengeance of the soul of Barnard' and the sudden shift of direction when the accumulated impression of decay is turned into the commercial slogan 'Try Barnard's Mixture' reflects a comic consciousness of something exaggerated in Pip's mood. Yet beyond that, there's the further notion of a sinister presence in Barnard's Inn practising a grim joke on the tenants, with its deeper appropriateness to Pip's story. This is the kind of thing Dickens meant in speaking of the 'tragi-comic conception' of the novel.

Comedy involves incongruity, and the key to Dickens's method is surprise. (Barnard's Inn, venerable and antique, suddenly becomes grotesquely up-to-date – Barnard's Mixture.) Here is a more light-hearted example:

> I found out within a few hours, and may mention at once, that Mrs Pocket was the only daughter of a certain quite accidental deceased Knight, who had invented for himself a conviction that his deceased father would have been made a Baronet but for somebody's determined opposition arising out of entirely personal motives – I forget whose, if I ever knew – the Sovereign's, the Prime Minister's the Lord Chancellor's, the Archbishop of Canterbury's, anybody's – and had tacked himself on to the nobles of the earth in right of this quite suppositious fact. I believe he had been knighted himself for storming the English grammar at the point of the pen, in a desperate address engrossed on vellum, on the occasion of the laying of the first stone of some building or other, and for handing some Royal Personage either the trowel or the mortar. (Chapter 23, p. 212)

The first surprise is whether 'accidental deceased Knight' means accidentally dead, or accidentally knighted. (We never really find out.) Then there is the fantasy that Mrs Pocket's grandfather ought to have been a Baronet, leading to the list of imaginary enemies who prevented it, ending in 'anybody' – you can hear the voice of Mrs Pocket's father mounting in paranoiac intensity, and Pip's in comic despair at the whole recital. We then arrive at the exploit for which the knighthood seems to have been conferred, 'storming the English grammar at the point of the pen', which combines the heroic notion of dauntless courage in the face of terrible odds with the painful and undignified fact that he couldn't write grammatical English. Finally, the last three words – handling the Royal Personage 'the trowel *or the mortar*'. Notice how Pip's understandably vague grasp of earlier details prepares us for a slight muddle on *his* part, before we realize that the confusion lay in the mind of Mrs Pocket's father, so totally absorbed in the nobility of the occasion that he made a mess of the actual ceremony. Or at least, that he *might* have made. To the end, he exists for us in a comic fantasy, which tells us better than any direct statement what to think about his, and his daughter's, genteel pretensions.

Now read the paragraph following the one just quoted. Look for examples of comic surprises of this kind.

DISCUSSION

The ones I notice are: (a) Mr Pocket who 'was . . . not quite decided whether to mount to the Woolsack, or to *roof himself in with a mitre*'; (b) the remark about taking time by the forelock 'when, to judge from its length, it would seem to have wanted cutting'; and (c) the sentences about Mr Pocket's wife being '"a treasure for a Prince". Mr Pocket had invested the Prince's treasure in the ways of the world ever since . . .' (pp. 212–13).

These are good examples of Dickens's usual way of working unexpected jokes into his writing. (a) illustrates a strong visual sense which momentarily provides a brilliant cartoon; while (b) and (c) show his fondness for taking some cliché or worn expression and, with a variation of his own, giving it satirical point. You will find other examples in Chapter 35 describing the funeral of Mrs Joe.

The problem about *discussing* comedy is that the jokes tend to get lost, or otherwise destroyed, by the labour of analysis. All I intend by these examples is to draw your attention to the way languge like this establishes the general tone of *Great Expectations*, its combination of sadness *and* humour. The fact that comedy is less easy to talk about doesn't make it any less vital to the total impression of the novel than effects from imagery, or extensively 'symbolic' writing. And to return to the question of 'realism', just as 'poetic' writing introduces into the narrative qualifying reverberations of meaning, so Dickens's comic writing has the effect of subverting and questioning the status of the world presented in terms of 'realism'. Barnard's Inn, or Wemmick's Castle, which we first meet in terms of Pip's direct observation, are also products of a play of language which link them to the tragic-comic conception governing the novel as a whole. We miss a key dimension of *Great Expectations* if we forget that such comic effects, products of the actual writing, amount to more than local displays of Dickens's inventive 'fancy'.

5. Interpretation Again

We have now considered *Great Expectations*, both formally and thematically, and debated some accounts of its meaning, or meanings. In this chapter, we will assume an overall familiarity with the text as a whole, in the way it achieves its effects and some 'main-line' interpretations of what these effects add up to, and on this basis, consider some undiscussed aspects of the novel, and some further interpretations arising from them. We have noticed that the accounts of 'Pip's Progress' outlined so far draw heavily upon the narrator's interpolated commentary on his younger self. Yet can these be altogether relied on? As I've already suggested, what the adult Pip tells us about the *significance* of his childhood development, is as much 'fiction' as that development itself, and equally subject to interpretation. Consider Pip's remark that he was 'morally timid' (Chapter 8, p. 92) as a consequence of his sister's manner of bringing him up. Or again, consider Herbert's answer to Pip's question: what kind of person had the one-time blacksmith's boy become? (Chapter 30, p. 269). Do such comments account for every thing we learn about Pip? Or does the text suggest further complexities and qualifications?

What is your view of the following brief episode? Pip, dismissed from his first interview with Miss Havisham, and treated contemptuously by Estella, begins to look round the deserted brewery.

> It was in this place, and at this moment, that a strange thing happened to my fancy. . . I turned my eyes – a little dimmed by looking up at the frosty light – towards a great wooden beam in a low nook of the building near me on my right hand, and I saw a figure hanging there by the neck. A figure all in yellow white, with but one shoe to the feet; and it hung so, that I could see that the

> faded trimmings of the dress were like earthy paper, and that the face was Miss Havisham's, with a movement going over the whole countenance as if she were trying to call to me. (Chapter 8, pp. 93–4)

'Fancy' is certainly one of Pip's characteristics, familiar to the reader, and rightly noted in Herbert's comment (Chapter 30, p. 269). But what does this particular exercise of 'fancy' convey to you? Here is another.

> On the edge of the river I could faintly make out the only two black things in all the prospect that seemed to be standing upright; one of these was the beacon by which the sailors steered – like an unhooped cask upon a pole – an ugly thing when you were near it; the other a gibbet, with some chains hanging to it which had once held a pirate. The man was limping on towards this latter, as if he were the pirate come to life, and come down, and going back to hook himself up again. (Chapter 1, p. 39)

The man in question is Magwitch, glimpsed by Pip on his way home from the meeting in the churchyard. What does this 'fancy' suggest? And do these two examples have anything in common which tells us something important about Pip? You will find a further clue in Pip's dream on the night before he steals food to take to Magwitch (see Chapter 2, p. 47).

DISCUSSION

We've seen that the young Pip is subjected to a good deal of physical knocking-about in these early chapters (from Magwitch, Mrs Joe, Pumblechook); of dismissive insult (from Wopsle, 'naterally wicious', p. 57), Pumblechook, Estella; and of obscure terror (Miss Havisham). His response to such treatment is usually reported by the narrator in that mildly ironic, sadly-humourous style which holds Pip's childish experience at a certain distance from us. And on the whole, Pip's overt behaviour is quiet, polite, pacific. But what the above 'fancies' surely reveal to us is a different reaction. In one case, Pip hallucinates Miss Havisham's death by hanging; in the other, he half-imagines the same for Magwitch. Such fantasy revenges upon two overbearing adult figures surely suggest that Pip's inner self, far from being polite and pacific, is (not at all surprisingly) unconsciously suffused with rage at the treatment he has been receiving. The clue in Pip's dream, which you may have noticed, lies in the notion that a ghostly pirate calls to him that he 'had better come ashore and be hanged there at once' (p. 47) on the gallows he had imagined Magwitch walking towards.

One prompting for this dream was Mrs Joe's scolding remark that boys who ask too many questions end up in the Hulks, laying the basis for Pip to identify himself with the convict. The dream further suggests that Pip's unstated anger against Mrs Joe, too immediately powerful a figure in his childish life to appear even as the target of a fantasy revenge, has to be directed against himself. A more explicit example of the tendency lies in his reaction to Estella's insulting behaviour. Pip has no other resource than, physically, to attack himself: 'so bitter were my feelings, and so sharp was the smart without name, that needed counteraction' (Chapter 8, p. 92).

It seems to me that such episodes imply an account of the young Pip that makes good psychological sense, enriching the adult narrator's moral version of his behaviour with an appropriate and convincing 'inner' dimension. There is then the further point that the adult narrator never consciously formulates or recognizes this 'inner' aspect of his childhood. His tale provides ample evidence, but he nowhere offers any interpretation of what it amounts to. This task develops wholly upon the reader. So our question is: does this aspect of the young Pip *contradict* what we might call the 'official' view sketched by the narrator, or does it just *complement* it? And if the latter, why does it get no 'official' recognition?

Perhaps you have already wanted to retort that the narrator is entirely explicit about the sense of guilt that haunts Pip's life at every stage? True enough, yet this is not the same as grasping its *causes*. We are told that Pip feels deep guilt at having stolen the food and file for Magwitch (Chapter 6). We also learn of his developing sense of social shame about his home and consequent ingratitude towards Joe (Chapter 14). Yet is it not also true that his guilt feelings take an inexplicably extreme form? When Miss Havisham gives Joe the money to pay for Pip's indentures as an apprentice blacksmith, Pip reports that the formal legal process of being 'bound' made him feel like a criminal, and appear so to others who are mere standers-by.

> I was pushed over by Pumblechook, exactly as if I had that moment picked a pocket or fired a rick; . . . I heard some people say, 'What's he done?' and others, 'He's a young 'un, too, but looks bad, don't he?' One person of mild and benevolent aspect even gave me a tract ornamented with a woodcut of a malevolent young man fitted up with a perfect sausage-shop of fetters, and entitled, TO BE READ IN MY CELL. (Chapter 13, p. 132)

The element of comic exaggeration doesn't conceal another implied self-identification of Pip with the criminal Magwitch, a link between them that recurs, in various contexts, throughout the story. Pip-as-narrator registers his younger self's guilty consciousness of ingratitude towards Joe because the apprenticeship that at one time had seemed the gate to adult freedom – or, as Joe puts it, 'larks' (p. 128) – has become a form of imprisonment. Yet the notion of criminality invites further interpretation. Pip's unconscious rage against his fate is so intense that, as in the dream we've looked at, it appears in the disguised form of fantasy punishment by the legally-constituted authorities. How else can we explain the implicit identification of Pip with a pickpocket, or rick-burner, or worse?

Will you now read through Chapters 15 and 16? What further evidence is there for the view that Pip's sense of guilt is of an intensity and depth as to require interpretation more searching than the narrator's mere consciousness that it existed? Don't forget that we need to look below the surface of Pip's state of mind, and to ask of the events he recounts what they imply and suggest.

DISCUSSION

There seem to me two notable pieces of evidence. Pip spends his half-holiday visiting Satis House, ostensibly to see Miss Havisham, in fact for a sight of Estella, to be greeted only with the news that she is being educated as a lady and the mocking question 'do you feel that you have lost her?' (p. 144). Returning home, he falls in with Wopsle who has just purchased a copy of a well-known play, a domestic tragedy called *The London Merchant, or the History of George Barnwell* (1731) by John Lillo (1693–1739).

Barnwell was apprentice to a merchant. Falling in love with the heartless courtesan Sarah Millwood, he robs his employer, and is encouraged by her to murder his uncle, for which crime both are imprisoned in Newgate Prison, tried and hanged. Wopsle recites the play to Pip, boring Pip to distraction yet also somehow contriving to identify Pip with Barnwell.

> Wopsle, too, took pains to present me in the worst possible light. At once ferocious and maudlin, I was made to murder my uncle with no extenuating circumstances whatever . . . and all I can say for my gasping and procrastinating conduct on the fatal morning, is, that is was worthy of the general feebleness of my character. Even after I was happily hanged and Wopsle had closed the book, Pumblechook sat staring at me, and shaking his head, and saying 'Take warning, boy, take warning!' as if it were a well-known fact that I contemplated murdering a near relation. . . (Chapter 15, p. 145)

It is not clear *how* Wopsle actually manages to read Barnwell's part so as to identify him with Pip, but this is what Pip felt about it; as indeed, does Pumblechook, who maintains his punitive, denunciatory role in Pip's young life. So, here again, Pip is identified with a criminal, one who goes to the gallows for murder.

The other evidence follows in Chapter 16 when Pip, his head full of George Barnwell, half-supposes that '*I* must have had some hand in the attack on my sister' (p. 147), and then, more seriously, finds that she had been struck down by the same convict's iron he had helped Magwitch to get rid of with Joe's file. 'It was horrible', he says, 'to think that I had provided the weapon, however undesignedly, but I could hardly think otherwise.' (p. 148). Surely this last feeling falls into the pattern of Pip's inexplicably intense feeling of irrational guilt? And would not the source of this guilt be that, as a child, he did experience murderous rage against his sister?

It is in these chapters that we first meet Joe's journeyman, Orlick. What did you make of him? What, in general, does he contribute to the novel? There is the suspicion that he might have struck down Mrs Joe, though his movements seem to give him an alibi (Chapter 16). Only much later does he admit to the crime (Chapter 53). He sees Pip as his favoured rival, which is odd, given that Pip and Joe are 'family'. He shadows Pip when he and Biddy go walking (Chapter 17), and seems to be a rival for her affections. He turns up at Satis House as porter and general handyman till Pip gets him dismissed (Chapter 30). Finally, he traps and nearly murders Pip, revealing that Compeyson is now his employer and that he knows all about Pip and Magwitch-Provis (Chapter 53, pp. 438–9). In 'plot' terms, this last function has its point: we know that Compeyson had set spies on Pip in order to catch Magwitch, yet could not any anonymous villian have served that purpose? Surely Orlick wasn't earlier introduced merely in order to provide Compeyson with an agent? Or is he introduced so that there *is* somebody to suspect of the attack on Mrs Joe? Again, surely any casual robber would have been sufficient? And what is the force of the strange affection Mrs Joe develops for Orlick after she has been attacked? It was, after all, Orlick who shouted that she was a shrew (p. 142). And lastly, why the final incident when Orlick nearly succeeds in killing Pip? One of his reasons for hating him must strike us, at the least, as surprising. Boasting of his attack on Mrs Joe, he says to Pip:

> I tell you it was your doing – I tell you it was done through you. . . I come upon her from behind, as I come upon you tonight. *I* giv' it her! . . . But it warn't old Orlick as did it; it was you. You was favoured, and he was bullied and beat . . . eh? Now you pays for it. You done it; now you pays for it. (Chapter 53, p. 437)

What did you make of this amazing statement, remembering the way Pip actually *was* brought up? We can see that Orlick has good recent grounds for hating Pip for having him sacked from his Satis House post. But his grudge has, it seems, this longer history and deeper root. What does all this contribute to the novel?

These questions take us back to our earlier discussion (see pp. 24ff.) of the way Dickens presents his characters. We meet Orlick in the 'external' mode. Why he is as he is, what his previous life was, how he thinks about himself and his actions, are as unexplained as similar questions about Pumblechook, and, for that matter, Mrs Joe. But of them, we can say that they carry a representative significance: they speak for the kind of society Pip grows up in. That is part of their role in the novel as a whole. But can we say that of Orlick? What is his relationship to the story? On the one hand, his behaviour and connection with Compeyson suggest that he belongs in the criminal underworld. Yet he is also a figure on his own, lurking in the margins of the story without that formal place in the social structure allotted to the other criminals – Magwitch, and his convict friends, the inhabitants of Newgate we meet through Wemmick. Did this lead you to think he was a kind of excrescence, more vividly present in the story than his plot-function merited, yet to no particular purpose? Julian Moynahan, in an influential article on *Great Expectations*, has argued that we should 'read' Orlick as a narrative *sign* of Pip's complex psychological state, a working out in terms of plot of those elusive suggestions about Pip's unconscious motivations and impulses that we have been discussing. We should think of Orlick as Pip's 'other self', his hidden psychological 'double', the character who embodies his hidden aggression against the powerful authority-figures who torment him in his childhood and block his path to advancement. Commenting on the scene in the lime-kiln, Julian Moynahan has this to say:

> The entire scene has a nightmare quality. This is at least partly due to the weird reversal of roles, by which the innocent figure is made the accused and the guilty one the accuser. As in a dream the situation is absurd, yet like a dream it may contain hidden truth. On the one hand Orlick, in interpreting Pip's character, seems only to succeed in describing himself – ambitious, treacherous, murderous, and without compunction. On the other hand, several of Orlick's charges are justified, and it is only in the assumption that Pip's motives are as black as his own that he goes wrong. We know, after all, that Pip is ambitious, and that he has repudiated his early associates as

> obstacles to the fulfilment of his genteel aspirations. Another interesting observation can be made about Orlick's charge that 'it was you as did for your shrew sister'. Here Orlick presents Pip as the responsible agent, himself merely as the weapon. But this is an exact reversal of Pip's former assumptions about the affair. All in all, Orlick confronts the hero in this scene, not merely as would-be murderer, but also as a distorted and darkened mirror-image. In fact, he presents himself as a monstrous caricature of the tender-minded hero, insisting that they are two of a kind with the same ends, pursued through similarly predatory and criminal means. This is what his wild accusations come down to.[1]

Moynahan goes on to suggest that Pip's story engages an archetypal childhood condition, brought about by the impotence of any child in relation to its parents, and by its irrational demand for unbounded love and admiration. Powerless to change its real conditions, the child creates a fictional world in which such 'great expectations' are fulfilled. Pip actually lives this fairy-tale solution to the problems of his own childhood, imagining a fairy godmother in Miss Havisham and that he is specially designed to be the beautiful Estella's lover. Magwitch's return brings him up against the reality of his situation and further locates the source of his wealth in the world of crime and violence, instead of the 'fairy' world of magically-fulfilled dreams. As to Pip's hidden aggressions, Moynahan points out that

> judged on the basis of what happens to many of the characters closely associated with him, Pip is a very dangerous young man. He is not accident-prone, but a great number of people who move into his orbit decidedly are. Mrs Joe is bludgeoned, Miss Havisham goes up in flames, Estella is exposed through her rash marriage to vaguely specified tortures at the hands of her brutal husband, Drummle. Pumblechook has his house looted and his mouth stuffed with flowering annuals by a gang of thieves led by Orlick. All of these characters, with the exception of Estella, stand at one time or another in the relation of patron, patroness, or authority-figure to Pip the boy or Pip the man. (Pumblechook is, of course, a parody patron, and his comic chastisement is one of the most satisfying things in the book.) Furthermore, all of these characters, including Estella, have hurt, humiliated, or thwarted Pip in some important way. All in some way have stood between him and the attainment of the full measure of his desires. All are punished.[2]

Think over this view of *Great Expectations*. See if you can formulate for yourself some reasons for finding it helpful, and also some objections to it.

DISCUSSION

I would suggest the following points in its favour. It makes good sense of the role of Orlick, which as we've seen, is not easy to account for. From the point of view of the main narrative. Orlick may be said, every now and again, to erupt with melodramatic effect (the attack on Mrs Joe, the attack on Pip), which nevertheless leaves a stronger impression than the narrative requires. But if he is considered as Pip's 'double', this impression is no longer superfluous, and also fits well with those recurrent glimpses we are offered of Pip's inner psychological state. We can then answer the question I raised on p. 73 as to whether this state complements or challenges the 'official' view of Pip as presented by the narrator. Moynahan's interpretation means that, for much of the narrative, Pip is deeply self-divided, or rather, that Dickens presents us with a self-consciously rational narrator whose story about his younger self implies a very different reality. As narrator, Pip remains unaware of those impulses in himself that resisted moral assimilation. Juxtaposed against the moral fable of 'Pip's Progress', which the narrator encourages us to construct, and of which Q. D. Leavis offers the fullest and most subtle statement, there is a less overt, yet discernible psychological fable. This is articulated partly through Pip's sense of irrational guilt (conscious trace of unconscious aggression), partly through the fairy-tale elements, complementing the surface narrative 'realism', in such characters as Miss Havisham and Orlick. These two accounts run in parallel, the moral one (as far as the narrator is concerned) largely sealed off from its psychological opposite. Yet both are accessible to the reader, providing a complex sense of the relationship between conscious morality and its less conscious psychological roots. Yet there is also an objection to Moynahan's interpretation. It has the effect of abstracting a psychological account of Pip's situation from a story presented within a well-defined social context. It hardly does Pip's childhood situation justice to derive his thirst for social advancement from an *archetypal* childish desire for unbounded parental love. His *only* source of affection is Joe, and as Joe himself admits (Chapter 7, pp. 78–80), he can only demonstrate his care for Pip within very strict limits. The commanding symbol of Pip's upbringing is surely Mrs Joe's aproned bosom, stuck full of pins and needles. The other adults surrounding his childhood are variously bullying, unjust, malicious, and – in Miss Havisham's case – cruel out of caprice, turning Pip into the instrument of her scheme for revenge on the male sex. Beyond these immediate personal contacts, there are the social and legal structures represented in the Hulks and Jaggers' world of Little Britain, uniformly represented as harsh and pitiless, especially towards the poor and the weak. Pip's childish dream of 'gentlemanly' ease and position thus takes shape within the particular context of this social world. Nor, as we have seen, are such ideas confined to him, but are shared in different terms by many other characters.

Bearing this in mind, we can return to the issue originally raised in Chapter 2, Pip's 'gentlemanly' aspirations, which we looked at very largely in terms of the text on its own. Yet, it doesn't take much thought to recognize that, for the novel's Victorian readers, such an issue had an immediate reverberation which the modern reader may not at first notice. Indeed, the paragraph cited from Humphrey House's essay (see pp. 43–4) describing Pip's story as 'a snob's progress', includes the point that the respectable Victorian work-ethic Pip eventually comes to share would have had Dickens's approval since it reflects directly the shape of the novelist's own career in which dedication to hard work had been pre-eminent (see the section entitled Biographical, pp 12–5). But Dickens was far from being the only Victorian reader who would have approved of Pip's work-ethic, and this wider 'contextual' aspect of *Great Expectations* deserves the modern reader's attention as Robin Gilmour has argued in his *The Idea of the Gentleman in the Victorian Novel* which devotes a substantial chapter to this aspect of *Great Expectations*. He notices that Pip's yearning for education and social advancement had a representative quality for those many Victorian readers for whom Samuel Smiles' influential book *Self Help* (1859) urged a wholly sympathetic group of ideals. Thus, 'self-culture' by means of improving reading was a specific recommendation of Smiles. As we have seen, Pip makes the point that despite his extravagant and wasteful London life, he stuck to his books. Self-culture, was the road to 'self-respect, dignity, the independence that comes from self-discipline . . . its end is character, not wealth or success.'[3] Pip's struggles in this direction evidently expressed a general social impulse that the novel directly addresses. Gilmour makes a further historical point, that the setting of the novel in the *early* nineteenth century was in itself significant.

> [Pip's] exaggerated allegiance to the concept of refinement is entirely characteristic of a culture which had barely emerged from the crude and violent society of the eighteenth century; the Victorians were proud, and rightly, of the improvements they had worked in the texture of daily living. . . The proximity to the Victorian age of a violent past, and the contrast which this made with the age's most

> treasured social achievements is of the utmost relevance to *Great Expectations*. On the one hand there is the England of 1860, relatively stable, relatively prosperous, conscious and rightly proud of the considerable advances in civilisation which the previous forty years had seen; and on the other there is the recent memory of a very different world, the harsh and brutal society of the eighteenth century which Victorian reformers set out to transform and which still survived as a background to their efforts — a source of congratulation but also of uncertainty and anxiety.[4]

As we have noticed, Dickens repeatedly underlines the inhumane ethos of Pip's world, especially shown in its treatment of the poor, the vagrant, the criminal and in the evidence of a brutal and dehumanising legal system.[5] You will recall that, newly arrived in London, Pip's first experience of the metropolis is the environment of Newgate, where a guide offers to show him the public whipping-place and the Debtor's Door through which would come those condemned to be hung (Chapter 20). Such details, Gilmour argues, had a historical specificity for Dickens's Victorian readers that we need to recapture if we are to do justice to Pip's search for a different quality of life. This historical perspective helps to explain the sense in which Satis House, in one respect a deadly influence on Pip's aspirations, has also its positive side, as was suggested by the imagery which links Miss Havisham and Estella to Pip's thoughts of freedom and hope (Chapter 15, and see p. 67).

When all is said and done, the life available to him in his home village, however virtuous an image of it we are offered in Joe and Biddy, is narrow and impoverished. And not only for Pip. Wopsle may be mainly a ludicrous figure, but he too has talents and aspirations of a kind and like Pip, Wopsle goes to London to try to realize them. Considered in this light, we can think of Wopsle's career as running parallel with Pip's; lacking Pip's good fortune, his 'expectations' come to nothing.

The novel's major irony turns, of course, on the fact that it is not Miss Havisham's inherited fortune, but Magwitch's wealth, won by hard and painful toil, that makes available to Pip the social advantages of educated society, agreeable manners, and cultivated living. Dickens thus enforces a connection between the real sources of wealth and the refined and respectable life which depends upon its possession, a fact about mid-Victorian middle-class life that Victorian readers would recognize, yet with the reluctance attached to awkward and disagreeable truths. You'll recall that Pip is horrified at any association between the 'beautiful young Estella, proud and refined' (Chapter 32, p. 284) and the criminal world of

Newgate Prison, yet we learn in the end that Estella is a child of Newgate. Pip, as it were, experiences in his own life the loathed, yet intimate, connection between the genteel and criminal worlds. Gilmour goes on to suggest that only when Magwitch's arrival in London forces Pip to abandon his illusions about the source of his 'gentility' are his positive energies released. Till that point, he has led a feeble and debilitated existence. But faced with Magwitch's dangerous presence in London, and accepting his responsibility towards him, the Pip of the novel's third part is transformed from the idle waster of the second. He develops a new tenacity and unexpected inventiveness in planning Magwitch's escape. He presses home his enquiry about Estella's real identity. He confronts Miss Havisham, appealing for help, not on his own, but on Herbert's behalf. And recalling Moynahan's argument about Orlick, we could say that he also confronts that part of his own being, hitherto suppressed, or articulated only as inner guilt, and emerges from the confrontation a more coherent and decisive personality.

Gilmour cites in support of this general view of Pip the account we have of him just before he begins the attempt to get Magwitch away from England.

> Wednesday morning was dawning when I looked out of the window. The winking lights upon the bridges were already pale, the coming sun was like a marsh of fire on the horizon. The river, still dark and mysterious, was spanned by bridges that were turning coldly grey, with here and there at top a warm touch from the burning in the sky. As I looked along the clustered roofs, with Church towers and spires shooting into the unusually clear air, the sun rose up, and a veil seemed to be drawn from the river, and millions of sparkles burst out upon its waters. From me too, a veil seemed to be drawn, and I felt strong and well. (Chapter 53, p. 444)

(If you turn back to our discussion of imagery (see above, p. 66–7) there is a detail to notice in this paragraph).

In sum, like Q. D. Leavis, Gilmour proposes that an 'integrated' mature Pip emerges at the end of the novel, but he adds a fresh social and historical context which gives Pip's growth and maturation a representative Victorian character. As with Moynahan's article, the above paragraphs only give the gist of Gilmour's general discussion, which should be directly consulted. Can you now, however, see an objection to it? Or at least, note that there is still more to be said about Pip's history?

DISCUSSION

Briefly, I suggest two points. Pip's new strength doesn't survive the capture and death of Magwitch, and only Joe's nursing care saves him from death. It's as if Pip's experience of embodying the social contradictions (crime/wealth: work/refinement) had been so damaging as to destroy his capacity for life. Then, there is the strange social limbo in which Pip's life ends. His only family life is by proxy – that of Herbert and Clara, or Joe and Biddy. And he now lives abroad. The hard-working, gentlemanly (in the good sense), middle-class business man seems to have no place in the society whose representative experience he carries (as it is Gilmour's case to argue). In the original conclusion, Pip meets Estella accidentally in London, she having married again, and happily, after the calamitous experience of her marriage to Drummle. Pip has little Pip with him, and Estella says: "'Lift up that pretty child and let me kiss it!' She supposed the child, I think, to be my child." (Appendix A, p. 496). But, as we know, the child isn't Pip's, but Joe's and Biddy's. Pip, in this version at least, will have no children of his own. The orphan who had to name himself remains, in the end, an outsider in the society that the story of his life has opened up for our contemplation.

There is, however, the published conclusion to the novel, suggesting a future for Pip and Estella, which we can best approach by way of a third account of *Great Expectations* provided by Peter Brooks in an article entitled 'Repetition, Repression, and Return: *Great Expectations* and the Study of Plot.'[6] But first let us consider here further the concept of 'plot' that we touched on in Chapter 2. How would you distinguish 'plot' from 'story'? And what aspects of *Great Expectations* would you use to illustrate these two terms? You could begin by considering the various meanings for 'plot' listed in a good dictionary.

DISCUSSION

The *Oxford English Dictionary* records three main meanings for 'plot': a plot of ground; a plan for a building, or chart, or literary work; a conspiracy, usually criminal (as in the Gunpowder Plot). We can discard the first; the second is clearly the one in question; but the third is worth noticing: 'plots' in plays or novels often do engage the illegal, the secretive, and the devious. The *OED* also provides this illustration for the second meaning: 'in every narrative work, there is a certain connection of events . . . which, in a work of fiction, is called a plot.' The key phrase here is *certain connection of events*. The connection in question is causality through time. Event A is found to have caused Event B; Event B caused Event C; and so to Event Z, the plot's conclusion. Time is involved because Event C cannot be thought to have caused Event A. Or rather, if that proved the case (as in a detective story where a clock has been tampered with to provide an alibi by disguising the true chronology of events), then Event C would be renamed Event A. Discovering a 'plot' often means tracing the correct chronology of causally-related events.

The 'plot' or 'plots' in *Great Expectations* are thus the sets of carefully-linked events flowing from Pip's contacts with Magwitch and Miss Havisham and forming that 'chain of iron or gold' (p. 101) that the story proceeds to reveal. Gradually these 'plots' are found to be mysteriously entwined, leading Pip (and the reader) to a knowledge of the master-plot worked by Compeyson, first on Miss Havisham and on Magwitch, long before Pip's story begins, then (via Orlick) on Pip himself, finally again on Magwitch. Reading for 'plot' involves the reader in a guessing-game as to which event belongs to, and reveals the nature of, the causal sequence that will eventually deliver the conclusion, and which events are actively misleading, or merely incidental. The ability to present episodes which can be read in different ways is at least one reason for Dickens's mastery of plotting technique. As you will recall from our discussion of Part I (see pp. 32 ff.), the reader is both encouraged to accept Pip's interpretation of the Havisham-plot, yet also provided with implicit counter-clues pointing to the Magwitch-plot.

What then of 'story'? If some events belong to 'plot', and some do not, is 'story' the term that includes both kinds? Yet we speak of 'telling the story of the novel', which suggests that by 'story' we mean another selection from its events than those providing the 'plot'. Consider again the narrative summary that we considered earlier (p. 39) for its adequacy as an account of 'theme', but now for its adequacy as 'story':

> *Great Expectations* tells the story of an orphan called Pip, harshly brought up by his elder sister, who is married to a blacksmith called Joe. One winter day, Pip meets an escaped convict in the churchyard near his home, where his parents are buried. The convict frightens Pip into stealing food for him, and a file to enable him to get rid of the irons on his leg. The convict is later recaptured. The following winter, Pip is introduced into the house of a rich eccentric spinster with a pretty niece, who makes him feel ashamed of his humble origins. Some years later, he is apprenticed to the blacksmith's trade, but dreams of becoming a gentleman and marrying the pretty niece. . .

Would you agree that this might pass muster as the 'story' of the opening chapters? Other versions are of course possible, and you could well contest this one as having omitted *key* events (Magwitch's assertion that he stole the food, the effect of Miss Havisham's appearance). Indeed, it's worth remembering that 'events' is also a problematic term that imposes its own implicit selections from the novel's verbal texture. Nevertheless, to contest the adequacy of the above 'story' as an account of the relevant chapters necessarily invokes the alternative concept of 'plot', since one event cannot be a 'key' except in terms of a significant *chain* of episodes. We can put this a different way by asking of the above 'story': where is it leading, what is its *point*? Its selection of events, unlike that of 'plot', yields no ready answer to that question, and indeed strongly resists its importunity.[7]

Let us test these definitions on a concrete example. Here is a paragraph from the novel you may have already looked at in another connection (see p. 66). Can you distinguish between elements of 'plot' and elements of 'story'? between significant and merely incidental detail?

> Mr Pumblechook's premises in the High-street of the market town, were of a peppercorny and farinaceous character, as the premises of a corn-chandler and seedsman should be. It appeared to me that he must be a very happy man indeed, to have so many little drawers in his shop; and I wondered when I peered into one or two on the lower tiers, and saw the tied-up brown paper packets inside, whether the flower-seeds and bulbs ever wanted of a fine day to break out of those jails, and bloom. (Chapter 8, p. 83)

DISCUSSION

Adopting our account of 'plot' as a set of causally-linked events, it is only when I read the final sentence (from 'and I wondered. . .') that I sense the presence of 'plot' in the form of Pip's characteristic habit of finding in his surroundings images of imprisonment that prompt 'fancies' of possible future release. Yet to interpret in this way is only possible because of the preceding sentences, and these seem to me pure 'story'. Nothing in the 'plot' requires that Pumblechook trade in corn and seeds. All the 'plot' demands is that he should trade in something, and had he been, like Trabb, an undertaker, would Dickens thereby have been prevented from giving Pip a comparable response? Surely not. . . In sum, we need 'story' if there is to be 'plot': we need details and episodes that are not closely linked in a casual sequence so that there will be others that are. The game that novelists play with us (have we seen, or have we missed, the signs of 'plot'?) depends on the presence of both kinds of event. This point has been formulated in general terms by Roland Barthes in his proposal that the forward momentum of narrative derives from an inherent ambiguity between mere 'consecutiveness' – episodes simply strung together in a chronological series as 'story' – and 'consequence' – episodes significantly linked in a 'plot'. Reading a novel is thus propelled by the search for 'consequence' as distinct from the aimless progression of 'consecutiveness'. We can relate this view of narrative to our previous discussion about interpretation (see pp. 40 ff.). Debates between rival interpreters repeatedly turn on whether details and episodes exist in the dimension of serial 'consecutiveness', or whether they can be differently arranged in the dimension of 'consequence', of these patterns of significance that interpretation necessarily seeks out. What we call 'a convincing interpretation' often depends upon its persuading us that seemingly casual or incidental detail can be differently seen within a pattern of significant interconnections. We began this chapter with just such a case – by looking at aspects of Pip's experience passed over in his account of 'consequence' in the events of his life, but which – considered more carefully – pointed to a hitherto ignored 'plot' about his inner psychological state.

In adopting 'causality' as the defining characteristic of 'plot', I have ignored a major difficulty (as perhaps you have noticed) – what *counts* as a 'cause' in the set of events laid out in a novel? We can, presumably, claim that Pip's chance meeting with Magwitch is a 'cause' in the way his life develops. While, at the other end of the scale, the fact that Pumblechook is a corn-chandler (as distinct from the fact that he is Miss Havisham's tenant) is not such a 'cause'. But what of Mrs Joe? Her 'bringing up by hand' powerfully influences Pip's development, as does the fact that Joe, having himself suffered and seen his mother suffer from a violent father, feels that only a pacific response to Mrs Joe's treatment of Pip is open to him. Should we not link this family background with the 'plots'? Then again, one over-arching 'cause' affecting all the characters is the punitive and hierarchical character of the society in which they find themselves living. Joe, you will recall, connects Mrs Joe with 'government' (p. 79). There are, in other words, causes upon causes, and the degree to which we see them as agents in the story will depend upon the assumptions – social, moral, psychological – that we bring to the novel, and in whose terms we *read in* the presence of active energies leading to the impingement of one event upon another. 'Plot', that is, is less an objective pattern to be uncovered (as the plan or 'plot' of a Roman villa, hitherto obscured by the debris of the centuries, might be uncovered by an archaeologist) than a product of interpretation shaped by initial assumptions about social and psychic life.

Peter Brooks's account of *Great Expectations* adopts such a conception of 'plot', which he derives from Freud's speculations in *Beyond the Pleasure Principle*. Brooks suggests that our need for and response to 'plot' in novels is rooted in our search for 'significant plots in our lives'. How, that is, do we impose structure and form on our experience of the endless – and pointless – flow of passing time? We do it by creating 'plots' that have (in the Aristotelian definition) a beginning, a middle, and end, whose individual episodes point to, and are consummated in, that end. In Freud's terms, the human 'plot' is structured by two conflicting principles: the self-preserving and pleasure-seeking life instincts (Eros), and the opposite, and in the end, dominating search for the inorganic quiescence of death (Thanatos) in a pattern peculiar to each organism. Thanatos thus provides the underlying structure from which Eros demands detours that nevertheless return to the end required by Thanatos. Brooks suggests that this model is reflected in the way 'narrative both seeks and delays its end'. He stresses the role of repetition in narrative as a means of pointing to, yet also postponing its own end, and thus conferring shape and significance on intervening 'plot' material. As a formal aspect of narrative, repetition is established by patterns of similarity within apparently different events. In discussing the 'themes' of *Great Expectations*, we have outlined examples of such repetition, for example, the recurrent identification of Pip and Magwitch. Brooks suggests that Pip's repeated returning to Satis House is such a pattern, engaging the conscious 'plot' of Eros in Pip's life (the pursuit and satisfaction of social and sexual desire), yet also pointing to the hidden 'plot', whose eventual emergence in the shape of Magwitch obliges Pip to confront a deeper repetition, 'the return of the repressed', his childhood identification with the criminal and the deviant. This, suggests Brooks, is the underlying 'real' plot of Pip's life which requires Pip to abandon the Eros 'plot' of his own desires for the Thanatos 'plot' which ends in the death of Magwitch and (we might add) in Pip's psychological 'death', represented in the illness he then suffers. Brooks comments:

> That it should be the criminally deviant, transgressive plot that is shown to have priority over all the others stands within the logic of the model derived from *Beyond the Pleasure Principle* since it is precisely this plot that most markedly constitutes the detour from

> inorganic quiescence: the arabesque of the narratable. One could almost derive a narratological law here: the true plot will be the most deviant. We might be tempted to see this deviant arabesque as gratuitous, the figure of pure narration. Yet we are also allowed to remotivate it, for the return of the repressed shows that the story Pip would tell about himself has all along been subverted by the more complex history of unconscious desire, unavailable to the conscious subject, but at work in the text. Pip has in fact misread the plot of his own life.[8]

This summary, as in earlier cases, does only limited justice to Brooks's essay, which should be directly consulted. But, in the quoted paragraph, do you notice an idea that we have already touched on? How would you distinguish this 'psychological' account of the novel from that of Julian Moynahan's? And is it open to the same criticism I suggested of Moynahan's?

DISCUSSION

To take these points in reverse order: like any primarily psychoanalytic account, Brooks's argument does disengage one aspect of the novel from its social context. This is usually entailed by any applicaton of Freud's later theorizing, which tends to assume the existence of an underlying human nature of which specific historical expressions are mere variants. But Brooks differs from Moynahan, in my view advantageously, by locating the psychoanalytic pattern within the structure of narrative itself. In a word, his discussion is more thoroughly 'textual', undertaking to connect our pleasurable interest in 'plot' with our own search for identity and significance. The point in the quoted paragraph that we have already touched on occupies the opening pages of this chapter: the narrator's failure to recognize what his story tells us about the inner psychological history of his younger self.

Brooks' argument further leads him to prefer the original to the published conclusion to the novel, on the grounds that Pip's 'real' story ends with Magwitch's death, so that any further relationship between Pip and Estella belongs to another novel. Will you now read over both conclusions and, in the light of the novel as a whole, consider which makes the more appropriate conclusion.

DISCUSSION

As Angus Calder points out, the original conclusion consorts better with Dickens's plan for the end of the novel. This notes that 'the one good thing [Pip] did in his prosperity, the only thing that endures and bears good fruit', was Pip's secretly arranging for Herbert to become a partner in Clarriker's. Pip's reward for his one good deed is to be provided with a secure niche in Herbert's firm, and (in effect) in his family. So (Calder proposes) to reward him further with marriage to Estella is to obscure this plain moral. Moreover, such a union can be seen as a sentimental concession to the demand for a happy romantic ending. Indeed, Dickens's own comment on the rewritten ending might suggest this. 'I have put in as pretty a little piece of writing as I could, and I have no doubt the story will be more acceptable through the alteration' (Appendix A, p. 494). But did you find anything substantial to be said on behalf of the published conclusion? I would make two suggestions. The first is that the merely 'moral' account of Pip's experience is not finally satisfactory; the moral judgements he elaborates throughout the story are more severe than the facts justify and need to be seen, in part, as symptomatic of the narrator's state of mind. The second is the substratum of fairy tale in *Great Expectations*, articulated in Miss Havisham and Magwitch, and in the 'poetic' dimension which, from time to time, the language of the tale opens up. This 'poetic' quality is very evident throughout the published conclusion, and the last paragraph explicitly evokes the scene that terminates 'The First Stage of Pip's Expectations' with the delicately allegorical reference to *Paradise Lost* we have noted (see p. 36).

> I took her hand in mine, and we went out of the ruined place; and, as the morning mists had risen long ago when I first left the forge, so, the evening mists were rising now, and in all the broad expanse of tranquil light they showed to me, I saw no shadow of another parting from her. (p. 493)

However, Brooks' argument that Pip's tale really ends with the death of Magwitch is not easy to counter, and perhaps some authorial consciousness of this accounts for the latent ambiguity of that last sentence which leaves us with two possible futures – that there *was* no other parting between them, but also that, for the moment, Pip did not *foresee* one. And a further point may be added. Happy marriage in Victorian novels signifies a final harmonious accommodation between the married couple and their society. I have suggested earlier that, socially speaking, Pip remains a shadowy figure, for whom society has no legitimate place. He cannot return to the forge and we cannot imagine him merely as another Herbert – his experience has been too complex and extraordinary. Yet, what other social place can he find that could do justice to that experience? The published ending satisfies on both counts. Its 'poetic' dimension invokes the essence of Pip's particular history and, as narrative, what it tells of pip and Estella's future remains suitably ambiguous.

But what was you own view of these alternative conclusions? Which seem to you to be the most satisfying — and why?

Notes

Chapter One: Contextual (Pages 1–16)

1 Cited in John Forster *The Life of Charles Dickens* (Chapman and Hall, 1872–74), Volume 3, p.328.
2 Op. cit., p. 329.
3 Op. cit.,p. 335.
4 Ibid.
5 Robert Garis *The Dickens Theatre: A Reassessment of the Novels* (Oxford University Press, 1965), p. 191.
6 Edgar Johnson *Charles Dickens: His Tragedy and Triumph* (Simon and Schuster, New York, 1952), Volume 1, p. 12.
7 Preface to the 1847 ed. of *Pickwick Papers*, quoted in John Butt and Kathleen Tillotson, *Dickens at Work* (Methuen, 1957), pp. 63–4.
8 For a detailed account of Dickens's practice as a serial novelist, see Butt and Tillotson, op. cit., pp. 14–34.
9 Butt and Tillotson, op. cit., pp. 15–16.
10 Philip Collins (ed.) *Dickens: The Critical Heritage* (Routledge and Kegan Paul, 1971), p. 516. The book can be generally consulted for its chronological survey of critical comment on Dickens's novels from the date of publication onwards. See the Index for references to *Great Expectations*.
11 Johnson, op. cit., Volume 1, p. 155.
12 F. R. and Q. D. Leavis *Dickens the Novelist* (Chatto and Windus, 1970), pp. 332–37.
13 Gordon S. Haight (ed.) *A Century of George Eliot Criticism* (Methuen, 1966), pp. 99–100.
14 Collins, op. cit., p. 264.
15 Letter to Mrs Brookfield (20 February 1866), *The Letters of Charles Dickens* (1880–82), Volume 2.

16 Forster, op. cit., Volume 3, p. 194. Forster's *Life* is, in general, a valuable account of Dickens's life and work. It is available in a two-volume edition, edited by A.J. Hoppé, (Dent, 1966).
17 Johnson, op. cit., Volume 2, pp. 991–2.
18 Forster, op. cit., Volume 1, Chapter 2.

Chapter Two: Formal (Pages 17–37)

1 For a fuller discussion of novelistic 'realism', see Chapter 4 and *Further Reading*.
2 Q. D. Leavis argues for a direct relationship. See her essay on *Great Expectations*, in *Dickens the Novelist*, pp. 320–1.
3 Watt, Chapter 1.
4 First published by Edward Arnold, 1927; page references are to the Penguin Edition of 1976.
5 G. H. Ford and L. Lane (eds) *The Dickens Critics* (Cornell University Press, Ithaca, USA, 1961), p. 52.
6 See Chapter 5.

Chapter Three: Thematic (Pages 37–54)

1 G. Robert Stange 'Expectations Well Lost: Dickens's Fable For His Time', *College English*, Volume 16, 1954–5, p 9.
2 For Dickens's view on Victorian education, see Philip Collins *Dickens and Education* (Macmillan, 1965).
3 Humphry House *The Dickens World* (Oxford University Press, 1941), p. 156.
4 Stange, op. cit., p. 18.
5 Leavis, op. cit., pp. 291, 313, 290.
6 Ibid, p. 313.

Chapter Four: Realism and Language (Pages 54–70)

1 See *Further Reading* on this issue.
2 In *Writing Degree Zero*, Roland Barthes criticizes the practice of nineteenth-century 'realist' novelists for failing to concede this gap between text and world.
3 Stange, op. cit., p. 16.
4 For another use of 'fire imagery', see Chapter 49, pp. 414–5. Does this fit the pattern?
5 John Carey *The Violent Effigy*, : *a study of Dickens's imagination* (Faber, 1973).

Chapter Five: Interpretation Again (Pages 71–89)

1 Julian Moynahan 'The Hero's Guilt: The Case of *Great Expectations*', *Essays in the Criticism*, Volume 10, 1960, pp. 66–7.
2 Op. cit., pp. 72–3.
3 Robin Gilmour *The Idea of the Gentleman in the Victorian Novel*, (Allen and Unwin, 1981), p. 122.
4 Op. cit., pp. 123–4.
5 For Dickens's keen interest in crime and the law in his own time, see Philip Collins *Dickens and Crime* (Macmillan, 1962), Chapter 1.

6 In *New Literary History*, Volume 11, No. 3, Spring 1980, pp. 503–25.

7 In arguing this distinction, I have drawn on and modified E. M. Forster's discussion of 'story' and 'plot' in *Aspects of the Novel*, Chapters 2 and 5. For a contemporary formalist approach to the topic, see S. Rimmon-Kenan *Narrative Fiction: Contemporary Poetics*, (Methuen, 1983), Chapters 2–3.

8 Op. cit., p. 516.

Suggestions for further reading

Great Expectations belongs to the latter phase of Dickens's career as a novelist, and the most relevant further reading to embark on now would be some of those other novels: the autobiographical *David Copperfield* (1849–50), much in Dickens's mind when be began *Great Expectations; Bleak House* (1853–3), which touches the theme of the blighting effect of 'great expectations'; *Little Dorritt* (1855–7) and *Our Mutual Friend* (1864–5). The last three titles, together with *Great Expectations* convey Dickens's developed ideas about Victorian society. They are all available in Penguin editions, as are most of Dickens's earlier novels. *Great Expectations* is also available in the New Oxford Illustrated Dickens (1857), though not yet in the authoritative scholarly Clarendon Edition (1966–) now in progress, also published by Oxford University Press. Norton Critical Editions, a series that includes with the text of the novel excellent notes, and a selection of useful contextual material and critical commentary, has a *Great Expectations* title, published by Norton, New York, 1965. For Dickens's biography and letters, see the titles listed in the notes to Chapter 1. Johnson's biography appeared in revised and abridged form in 1977 (Allen Lane). Another single-volume biography worth knowing about is *Dickens: A Life* by M. and J. Mackenzie (Oxford, 1979). There is a three-volume edition of Dickens's letters, edited by Walter Dexter (Nonesuch Press, 1938). A modern Collected Letters, the Pilgrim Edition, is now in progress, edited by Madeline House, Graham Storey, and Kathleen Tillotson (Oxford, 1965–).

For articles on *Great Expectations* other than those discussed in the *Guide* see Norman Page (ed) *Dickens: 'Hard Times', 'Great Expectations', and 'Our Mutual Friend': A Casebook* (Macmillan, 1980). For a detailed analysis of the texts of the two endings and a survey of their subsequent critical discussion, you could consult Edgar Rosenberg's article in *Dickens Studies Annual*, Volume 9, 19780. John Kucich discusses 'Action in Dickens Endings: *Bleak House* and *Great Expectations* in *Nineteenth Century Fiction*', Volume 33, 1978.

A number of general books on the novels include stimulating chapters on *Great Expectations*. In *The Moral Art of Dickens* (Athlone, 1970), Barbara Hardy focuses on that central Dickension theme of the giving/withholding of food in the novel. Dennis Walder in *Dickens and Religion* (Allen and Unwin, 1981), an analysis of the role of religious ideas and images in several novels, includes some pages on *Great Expectations*, noting the underlying pattern of sin, repentance and regeneration. Taylor Stoehr in *Dickens: The Dreamer's* Stance (Cornell University Press, Ithaca, New York, 1965) analysing Dickens's narrative strategies as a form of dream, includes discussion of *Great Expectations* from this angle. Robert Garis' *The Dickens Theatre: A Reassessment of the Novels* (Oxford, 1965), offers an account of the novel drawing on Freud's *Civilisation and its Discontents*, and Steve Connor in *Dickens* (Blackwell, 1985) makes use of Lacanian psychoanalytic ideas (which combine Freudian psychoanalytic theory and Saussurean linguistics), devoting some pages to the novel. For the role of fantasy and fairy tale in *Great Expectations*, see Harry Stone *Dombey, David Copperfield and Great Expectations* (Macmillan, 1981). General works on Dickens's novels are so prolific that any small selection must seem arbitrary, but in addition to the above, you could turn to Alexander Walsh *The City of Dickens* (Clarendon Press, Oxford, 1971) which examines the role of the city, both real and ideal in the novels, and shows how the presentation of London in *Great Expectations* reveals links with Dickens's work as a whole. *Dickens and the Rhetoric of Laughter* (Clarendon Press, 1971) by James R. Kincaid, though not treating *Great Expectations* in detail, provides a helpful approach to the novel's comic aspect. Susan R. Horton in *The Reader in Dickens: Style and Response* (Macmillan, 1981) analyses the range and variety of style in Dickens's writing, with enlightening implications for the styles of *Great Expectations*. On the subject of the presentation of women in Dickens's novels, see Kate Flint's *Dickens*, Chapter 6 (Harvester, in press). On the issue of 'realism', there is a valuable introductory account by J. P. Stern *On Realism* (Concepts of Literature), (Routledge and Kegan Paul, 1973). Classical works such as Eric Auerbach's *Mimesis: The Representation of Reality in Western Literature* (Translated by Willard R. Task), (Princeton University Press, 1953), and Georg Lucáks' *Studies in European Realism* (trans. E. Bone, Merlin Press, 1972), can be consulted. The critique of this general position, which developed as a result of structural linguistics and the influence of Saussure, is represented for the new reader in a number of readily-available titles: *Critical Practice* by Catherine Belsey (Methuen, 1981), Ann Jefferson and David Robey (eds) *Modern Literary Theory: A Comparative Introduction* (Batsford, 1982), Terence Hawkes *Structuralism and Semiotics* (Methuen, 1977), Terry Eagleton *Literary Theory* (Blackwell, 1983). All these titles contain valuable select bibliographies.

Index